Eastern Philosophy, Western Talk

A Guide To Understanding Body Energy

JESSICA BLACKBOND

Copyright © 2024 Jessica Blackbond

All rights reserved.

ISBN-13: 9798335500890

DEDICATION

My heart, Ralph.

CONTENTS

Introduction — Page 6

Wisdom — Page 11
The Third Eye Chakra, Pituitary Gland, Pineal Gland, Cervical Region Energy Zone, Tripple Burner and Pericardium Channels, Celestial Energy Field.

Ego — Page 37
The Sacral Chakra, Oestrogen and Testosterone, Lumbar Region Energy Zone, Kidneys and Bladder Channels, Emotional Body Energy Field.

Unity — Page 66
The Root Chakra, Adrenal Glands, Pelvis Region Energy Zone, Stomach and Spleen Channels, Etheric Body Energy Field.

Power — Page 95
The Solar Plexus Chakra, Pancreatic Glands, Lower Leg Energy Zone, Heart and Small Intestine Channels, Mental Body Energy Field.

Reflection — Page 125
The Heart Chakra, Thymus Gland, Thoracic Region Energy Zone, Lungs and Large Intestine Energy Channels, Astral Body Energy Field.

Balance — Page 154
The Throat Chakra, Thyroid Glands, The Throat Energy Zone, Liver and Gall Bladder Energy Channels, Etheric Template Energy Field.

Akasha — Page 179
Crown Chakra, Hypothalamus Gland, Ketheric Body Energy Field.

mind, you are listening to my brain. I hope this interpretation of my learning, discovering, and understanding of Eastern philosophies can help to sprout your seed of knowing who you are and begin a journey of exploring what your life is about.

This book describes 'body energy'. The content is purely focused on relaying combined concepts from aeons old Chinese and Indian philosophies that have travelled throughout time across oceans and continents to the West, where spoken words were transcribed to writing and became world-wide 'knowing'.

I have intended that each story throughout the book gives an overview of your body energy systems: chakras, energy zones, energy channels, and energy fields. Within each chapter I explain how being aware of the balance between each can create harmony of internal and external mind, body and soul responses. With diagrams and self-help exercises throughout I have made the content easy to follow so you are gaining an easily doable holistic approach to improving your vibrant wellbeing, starting today.

Information in this book is not meant to be medically prescriptive, nor is it philosophy of physics, mathematics, or theology; although during the research stage of collecting information I did melt my own brain going down a rabbit hole and finding myself studying the theology of Jesus, who by the way is believed by yogis to have been a yogi himself. But that is not relevant for this book.

Body energy is something that we can all relate to, we all feel it, we can understand it, and we can all access the power of it if we attune and balance our vibrational matrix, just as ancient civilisations did long, long ago....

INTRODUCTION

Once upon a time I sat with a yogic monk. A shift happened within me after meeting him. He hosted a group of talks where guidance was offered on how to get deep into the root of who we are, giving me an opportunity to really self-reflect.

That typical question I struggled to answer "Who am I?"

A 72 year old man with a white beard down his chest, and the cutest giggle laugh. He asked us questions and waited for an answer, even when the uncomfortable silence came, he waited for an answer. What a man. To conclude each talk we were invited to ask questions. I remember one person asking a question, and the yogic monk giving an answer. The person then silently left the room, disappointed.

Another person asked "What will happen now he has left?" The yogic monk replied "The fact that he was interested to attend here today means that somewhere in his mind there is a seed of knowing who he is and what his life is about. Not what he learnt in school, or what is on the tv or in the news. No. A seed of knowing his true nature that wants to be discovered and nurtured. The fact that he has left means that the seed has started to sprout. No matter if he tries to forget, sooner or later that will manifest in awakening."

The impact of this short speech resonates with me still today. The power of knowledge is truly mysterious. It affects us emotionally and physically because we are whole human beings connected to everything around us… and everything is connected to everything!

We are together in this. As you absorb my writing into your

ACKNOWLEDGMENTS

Thank you to all the people who have given advice and support when discussing body energy, and big thanks to those who have encouraged and celebrated the development of this book.

I most heartedly want to thank all the people who have supported the gradual development of Holistica, an alternative massage school with Eastern inspired quality teaching, where regular workshops and events in well-being and self-care are held. For more information on Holistica Training Centre visit www.holistica.org.uk.

Gratitude goes to the yogic monk in Himachal Pradesh, Dharamsala who gave me inspiration to look deeper into my own body energy.

The ancient Chinese philosophers observed the natural world as a balance and harmony of opposite forces. If it was cold in one place, it was hot in another. If the sun shone during the day, it was the moon that ruled at night. Masculine energy and feminine energy. Opposites in balance. These observations, based on a search for inner harmony in direct relationship with the harmony of nature that surrounded the ancient folk, became the basis of Taoism. The teachings of Traditional Chinese Medicine were eventually documented in a 237BCE text called The Nei Ching (The Yellow Emperor's Classic of Internal Medicine).

Civilization in the Indus Valley of ancient India gave rise to Ayurvedic Medicine and the knowledge of the human condition, the universe, and of the people's place in it. Compiled as 'The Vedas', the Rig Veda became one of the most sacred and oldest books of human history, dating back to around 1500 BCE. Raja Yoga, the uniting of opposites in balance, is considered a main part of the writing. The Vedas were based on Hindu traditions that were verbally handed down by ancestors telling tales and stories of peace, unity, and of the source of all creation.

And across the globe, healing systems and philosophies followed the same understanding: that vibrations from a higher consciousness interacts with vital life force vibrations to make all living organisms work efficiently and with optimum wellness. Hermetic philosophy of the ancient Greeks and Egyptians covered temple walls in hieroglyphs often representing the 'magic' of the vibrational matrix that stands behind everything in the physical world, including the physical body.

It is only in the last couple of hundred years that the aeons old traditions of internal energy healing has become manipulated into a 'quick fix'. Today Western science and medicine tend to look at the physical body directly; with specialists waiting lists and prescribed medications. Sadly the knowledge and awareness of the ancient holistic approach to mind, body, and soul wellness have been, mostly, overlooked.

Fortunately, Eastern energy workers continue the legacy and are passionate to spread the understanding once again. I am blessed to have met some of the energy workers and I am grateful to have experienced and witnessed first-hand what happens when the opposing energies balance and the body realigns to a state of harmony and gentle rhythm.

This book explains some of the ancient Eastern philosophers' holistic approaches that I have categorised into seven sections: Wisdom, Ego, Unity, Power, Reflection, Balance, and Akasha. I find it fascinating that these ancient Eastern philosophies are as relevant to today's living standards as they were aeons ago and, as the yogic monk I sat with said, they can sprout the seed of knowing your true nature that wants to be discovered…

What is Body Energy?

Prana Energy: External light from the universe, sun, and stars that enters your body through the third eye.

Qi Energy: Internal energy that holds your body's structure strong against the pull of gravity. It travels through all energy channels and is stimulated by movement.

Jing Energy: Internal energy absorbed from food and water. It feeds your body's organs with metabolic energy to pump blood, digest food, excrete waste, and enable the senses.

Chakras: Spinning wheels that control the internal circulation of body energy. Located throughout your body, however the main seven are located along your spine.

Energy Channels: The pathways for internal energy to flow to and through your body's organs and endocrine glands.

Energy Fields: Your body's aura made up of many interconnected layers of coloured light transmitting information between your chakras and your body's surrounding environment to communicate your internal energy (thoughts, feelings, and experiences).

Body Organs: Your main organs are your brain, heart, small intestine, lungs, large intestine, liver, gall bladder, kidneys, bladder, stomach, spleen, pancreas, and skin.

Hormones: Your endocrine system is a messenger system of natural chemicals that are secreted by glands connected to your organs. The messages are released into your bloodstream to feedback to your brain for maintaining optimal body wellness.

Wisdom

Connecting the Third Eye to the Mind
The Identification of Internal and External Influences

The Third Eye, The Pituitary Gland, and The Pineal Gland
Cervical Region Energy Zone
Tripple Burner and Pericardium Channels
Celestial Energy Field

Do not underestimate the effect your internal world has on your external vibrations. All is Mind. And the Mind is Wisdom.

Connecting the Third Eye to the Mind

We are starting off with a short physics lesson in vibration, because vibration is the foundation of everything, and everything is connected.

The principle of vibration is simple: Everything moves. Everything oscillates. Everything shifts from one place to another and back again. The speed or rate at which something vibrates is referred to as it's frequency.

Natural energy derives from source: that being the universe, the sun and the stars. Energy from source covers everything, and this energy is not still. It dances constantly at a frequency believed to be 432hz. Hz (Hertz) measures the number of oscillations in one second. The way I understand this is by imagining I stand next to a wall, I throw a ball against the wall. The ball moves from me, bounces off the wall, and returns to me. This action is one oscillation.

The vibrational frequency of earths energy from source is made of 432 bounces in 1 second, or 432 oscillations in a one second cycle. When living organisms resonate with a frequency of 432hz the body feels and radiates calm. As a result the mind becomes attentive to listen and observe in quietness. This frequency state is perfect for meditation, deep thought, or observing the thoughts come and go without any attention to them.

However, it is very difficult for us contemporary humans to operate at this level. We are surrounded by and made up of billions of molecules, atoms, sounds and smells from other living organisms which are constantly vibrating at many different frequencies. You see, the environment and everything in it also vibrates: machinery, vehicles, movements, electronic devices, air (affected by weather, temperature, and quality) are all varying energies that enter the body as information through the mind - the third eye to be exact, where interaction with wisdom takes place.

"What is wisdom?" I intuitively sense from you. Well, wisdom gives you the awareness, knowledge, and intelligence of making mindful judgements based on previous experience in order to think, respond, and react calmly. Known by names such as sixth sense, intuition, déjà vu, extrasensory perception etc.

Your internal body energy naturally vibrates at frequencies ranging from 396hz – 963hz at different sections throughout your body's structure. Each energy field, which surrounds your physical body, processes the random energy, manipulates the vibrations to match the corresponding chakra frequency, which then directs the energy to travel to energy zones through each associated energy channel to the connected body organs where related hormones are released, resulting in mind and body reactions and projected vibrations. Don't worry if this has blown your mind - I'll go through them in detail shortly.

Depending on how well your processing system is functioning, balanced or blocked energy is projected out into the world through your actions, thoughts, feelings, and speech. And that energy is always reflected back at you. So if you find yourself asking "Why is life always so XYZ?" it is likely your internal energy is making life so XYZ.

The ancient Eastern philosophers prescribe the practice of allowing time to question "How and why am I feeling this reaction?", while being mindful of your body's internal frequencies resonating with the external frequencies, which combined regulate your 'scattered mind' from a lack of control.

A great example of this: Imagine you are with a group of people together in a space. The energy of the environment and the energy of the group of people is not something you can see or touch, but it is something you can sense, feel, and react to. Isn't it interesting that you intuitively know who you are vibing with, and who you should probably avoid. But sometimes this instinct can be off, and you can find yourself in complete disharmony with the group. How you process the vibrations and how your body responds to the different frequencies shows how attuned to your wisdom you are, and ultimately how your entire experience is affected.

The Identification of Internal and External Influences

I had known of Alastair for many years before meeting him. Alastair is a successful, extremely busy, and well known business man in the North of England. He is in his mid-40's, married, and has two grown children.

I was recommended to Alastair for massage therapy at his home from a client who knows him well. Our first meeting started like this:

Me: "Hi, it's Jessica for your massage."

Alastair: "Jessica. I'll open the gates love. Come on down to the house."

As I drove into the parking area I could see Alastair waiting for me outside the house entrance. I was instantly amazed at how large he is. I most definitely do not mean large by weight, I mean large by his physique and the way he held himself: strong and muscular with a refined self-assurance. I started giggling to myself as he walked closer to my car signaling to me where to park, much like an aircraft marshaller does when signaling to the pilot to keep turning, slow down, and stop the airplane. I parked and jumped out of my car.

Alastair: "What did you think coming down the lane? I bet you thought where the chuff is this taking me, eh? "

Alastair spoke with a strong Yorkshire accent along with a proper Yorkshire tongue in cheek humour. I immediately liked his vibe.

As we began our walk into his home, and as I set up the massage equipment, Alastair chatted easy going conversation with me, and with focused eye contact he asked me general questions that he appeared genuinely interested to hear the answers to. During the consultation he told me that he lived life fast and hard. "I'm in it 100% or I'm not in it at all, Jessica. That's how I get things done." He also told me that as soon as he meets someone, he likes to look directly into their eyes. He said his intuition can work them out that way, and he is 99% of the time accurate in his perception.

"Interesting" I thought. "Very interesting. Alastair knows exactly what he wants out of life." And I knew I was going to enjoy this connection.

Throughout the years of visiting Alastair at his home we have had a lot of fantastic conversations. He remembers previous discussions and can regularly refer back to them with clear memory and factual detail. It is fabulous how we can leave a conversation half way through and then pick it up on our next meeting. Alastair visualises ideas while he speaks, and he communicates them by using his hands, often with gestures or through images that he can quickly find on his phone.

One of the qualities I admire about Alastair is that he is very seldom unhappy. Even when his world around him is throwing challenges in his direction he seems to rise above it with an ability to recognise a meaning to the situation. His strong memory of the past can find patterns from previous experiences which he then uses to invoke a positive outlook.

It wasn't until an out-of-the blue question from Alastair that I realised the incredibly obvious.

Alastair: "Have you ever thought about opening a massage shop, Jessica?"

Me: "Erm…. It is funny you say that actually. I have recently been thinking of my dream to teach massage with body energy and body posture awareness. It is so far out of my remit though."

Alastair: "Why do you say that. I know you will make it work. Do it"

There and then it dawned on me… Alastair's third eye is well and truly open:

√ Alastair knows what he wants out of life and follows his strong intuition.

√ Wisdom allows him to recognise patterns from which he can create meaning and consciousness to everyday life.

√ He has a really good memory of the past with factual detail.

√ He experiences a strong perception of his surroundings.

√ He is able to think symbolically and is able to visualise concepts, ideas, and other peoples dreams and ambitions.

The more I get to know Alastair, the more I can clearly see his third eye energy. And the brilliance is that Alastair also knows when the power of his third eye is blocked - his mind becomes predominantly controlled by his sensory perceptions, what Alistair calls his 'knee jerk reactions'. For example, he will notice he mirrors the energy surrounding him and as a result he becomes quick to respond. Sometimes this can be speaking and behaving in ways that are completely out of his character. He will notice he is eating far more sugary foods than usual, and he finds himself instinctively wanting to visit a tree close to his home, at the top of a hill where he can sit alone while he 'tries to work himself out'.

When there is this contrast of energy frequencies throughout his body, Alastair's wisdom and knowledge does not function efficiently. Alastair tells me he notices that he is 'off the rails', his sleep becomes disturbed, he can latch on to ideas and create obsessions which can make it difficult to concentrate on anything else. His 'live life fast' philosophy is basically an outlet for when his energy at the third eye is too excited.

The Third Eye, The Pineal Gland and The Pituitary Gland

The third eye chakra represents identity, insight, intuition, self-reflection, and the act of seeing – both physically and intuitively. It allows us to see clearly, letting us observe the big picture.

All energy in the environment, including conversations, vision, sound, actions and movements, touch, smells, and temperature is absorbed into your physical body through the third eye, in the centre of your forehead in-line with your eyebrows. This absorbed energy is constantly vibrating in a chaos of frequencies as it travels directly into the centre of your brain. The vibrating energy then travels down your spine, where energy is dropped off at five specific 'energy houses' known as chakras, all the way to the tail bone. Each chakra rotates the absorbed energy like a spinning wheel, transforming the absorbed energy's frequency to match its own frequency and then releases the balanced energy in an upward direction towards the top of your head where it enters your mind. If all is well within your chakra system your mind becomes 'open'. It is said that when the mind is open wisdom is available and the soul becomes illuminated - there is harmony and control of perception, thoughts, speech, and behaviour.

However, if there are problems at any part of your chakra system, often due to poor diet, stress, over thinking, not enough sleep, lack of physical exercise, or overindulgence, both negative and positive, then the opposing external and internal energies cannot balance, which results in energetic chaos - the faculty of wisdom cannot be accessed and therefore 'unfiltered' thoughts, speech, and behaviour occurs. Your perception of the world around you becomes unclear.

The third eye is the 6th chakra within your chakra energy system. Also known as the Brow Chakra and Ajna, it is energetically connected to the base of your brain where the pituitary gland and pineal gland are situated, behind the bridge of your nose. The pituitary gland is about the size of a small pea. Given its tiny size, it plays a huge role in keeping your body working well. Known as The Master Of Glands, the pituitary gland senses when your body is in need and immediately sends signals to the other hormone releasing glands throughout your body to release the natural chemicals required to keep you and your body working efficiently. Five of these main hormones are:

Adrenocorticothrophic Hormones (ACTH): Stimulates and controls the adrenal cortex, the fight or flight mechanism.

Follicle-Stimulating Hormones (FSH): Plays a key role in sexuality and fertility (oestrogen, progesterone, and testosterone).

Growth Hormones: Controls bone and muscle growth, and maintains the body's structure and energy production (metabolism).

Thyroid-Stimulating Hormones (TSH): Controls the growth and activity of the thyroid gland which affects metabolism, energy levels, and the nervous system.

Anti-Diuretic Hormones (ADH): Helps the kidneys manage the amount of water in the body.

The pituitary gland has a feedback mechanism linked to the pineal gland, which also has a major job to do in keeping your body's energy balanced, your mind open, and your soul enlightened.

Have you ever noticed the pine cone used in many ancient relics and symbols of Hindu cultures, Asian cultures, Egyptian cultures, and many other cultures throughout history? The pine cone carries a significant meaning of knowledge and wisdom and also represents the third eye. And guess what the pineal gland looks like… a tiny pine cone (approximately 0.8cm in size).

The pineal gland releases the hormone melatonin. Melatonin plays a crucial role in regulating your sleep-wake patterns known as the circadian rhythm. It helps you maintain regular and restful sleep patterns. You know when you are so tired your brain starts to play tricks on you - you don't think straight, you are irritable, and you just want to cry? That's when the energy frequency at your third eye is not balanced to 852hz (that's 852 bounces in 1 second).

As we've seen (pun intended), the third eye is associated to your vision of everything, including visualisation of your own desires, ambitions and even dreams. When energy imbalance is prolonged, extreme signs and symptoms of third eye chakra and the pineal gland energy imbalance can show as:

- anxiety or depression
- hair loss
- low energy
- decreased memory
- sinus headaches
- hearing loss
- eye problems

Before any of these symptoms present, psychological emotions arise to warn us of an energy imbalance, often shown as:

- self-doubt
- distrust
- poor ability to observe objectively

- closed off in imagination
- speech and behaviour can become insensitive
- you find difficulty in knowing what to do or how to make decisions
- imagining the future is challenging
- you experience a feeling of isolation from others

The ancient Eastern philosophers spoke of practical solutions to balance the frequencies at the chakras. At the third eye, remedies include surrounding yourself with the colour indigo or purple and burning a candle of lavender, fir, or chamomile fragrances to ease your senses. Dedicating the light of the candle to the well-being of yourself and to heal what needs to be healed can bring more clarity and peace of mind. Truth and knowledge activates this chakra. Immersing yourself with violet and hyacinth flowers brings a sense of happiness, and placing fluorite, amethyst, or azurite crystals in the palm of your hand can release calming energy. Eating purple coloured foods such as blueberries, dark chocolate, lavender, and grapes are believed to cleanse the third eye.

But of course not everyone is inclined to practise these remedies, nor is it always possible. There is good news though... there are other ways to balance internal frequencies, beginning with how you hold yourself.

Cervical Region Energy Zone

Contemporary living has exposed humans to a massive spectrum of chaotic external vibrational frequencies from the use of computers, machinery and vehicles, smart phones, television, internet, social media etc. As we have just discovered, external vibrations interact with internal body vibrations and can, as a result of over exposure to frequency imbalance, interfere with your body energy efficiency. It can also cause body discomfort.

Generally, in current Western society, we have become burdened and constantly bombarded with challenging information which makes the third eye very busy, and when this happens the physical body feels it. Imbalance at the third eye is felt at the head and neck area – literally the feeling of 'carrying the weight of the world on the shoulders'.

Let's get scientific again with physiology this time...

The trapezius is a massive muscle across both sides of your upper back and neck area. It is the most common muscle to hold energy tension. The trapezius runs from the base of your skull, down your neck, across the top of your shoulders to the very edge of the shoulder joints where you can feel a V shape at the end of your collar bones. At this area the muscle naturally separates. One part runs around the front of your shoulder joint, under your armpit and inserts at the outer side of your upper arm, just underneath the deltoid muscle. The other part runs diagonally from the V at the collar bones, under the shoulder blades towards your spine, where it inserts into the middle and upper vertebras.

Muscles are made up of many, many fibres. In secondary

school education we are told 'Physical movement occurs when muscle fibres contract and extend as a result of chemical energy transforming into mechanical energy.' and 'Blood carries oxygen from the lungs to all parts of the body to feed muscles.' But we are not informed of the muscle fibre waste product Lactic Acid, which is the chemical made when muscle movement and oxygen is combined. Lactic acid is transported from the muscles, carried in the bloodstream, and is eliminated as part of the body's waste process. This, I believe, is massively important for understanding why we feel aches and pains when we are tired, and what we can do to re-energise.

Normally the level of lactic acid in your blood stream is low. When you are tired, both psychologically and physically, your body responds with shorter breaths resulting in lower levels of oxygen in the bloodstream and therefore a relatively higher level of lactic acid. Because lactic acid is a waste product, having high levels in the blood creates a toxic environment. But your body wants to be in good health, so your muscles immediately respond by pausing the release of lactic acid into the bloodstream. The pituitary gland now kicks in with the production of Adrenocorticothrophic Hormones (ACTH) stimulating the adrenal gland cortex to release adrenaline and cortisol hormones – your fight or flight response. These hormones tell your muscles to be ready for physical movement. But there is a problem - your muscles have lost the ability to contract and extend efficiently because the lactic acid is trapped in the muscle, and so to protect the muscle tissue, the muscle goes into constant contraction. The muscle's fibres remain short, the lactic acid becomes stagnant in your muscle, and your body begins to ache.

Phew. Did you get that? Basically if energy at your third eye is not balanced, stress becomes present, your body responds and the trapezius muscle begins to ache. Quite often this is projected as a 'pain in the neck'.

Ancient Eastern philosophers say you should focus on the body. When over chaotic energies from the outside world penetrate your inner world, and if you do not focus on healing the body, the whole harmonised energy process does not work and sight of what it would take to correct the chaos is lost. By practising body posture movements that open the spine, styles such as tai chi, qi gong, hatha yoga, and asana yoga, you can release the burden in the third eye. Although it is not always possible to do these techniques, it is possible to stretch. Here is a great posture stretch to release the shortened trapezius muscle and open your spine. I do this every time I make a cup of tea:

Pull tall through the crown of your head: Imagine that your spine is a pearl necklace extending from the top of your head right down to your tailbone. You don't want the pearls to touch so you need to pull the string at the crown of your head up, standing taller with your chin pulling back to make a nice double chin, and to open the base of your skull. Keep looking ahead – not down to the floor. At the same time, pull the string at your tailbone to lengthen towards the heels of your feet, opening the space between each pearl throughout your spine.

Throughout my 20+ years of body movement therapy work I have seen this posture stretch almost immediately reflect higher self-esteem, a better mood, and lower levels of stress response. It really is incredible how powerful body awareness can be. And the foundation of powerful body awareness is good alignment of the energy system channels.

Tripple Burner and Pericardium Channels

Prana energy is the energy behind all movement in the universe. Mysteriously, prana energy cannot be seen, but it can be sensed and its flow can be changed through human-to-human connection, such as through massage and an awareness of others' projected energy. It is the source of warmth, it is the basis behind the transformation of your emotions, and it governs your connection to everything surrounding you. Prana energy is known as the Lateral Circulation. It comes from the environment and passes through your body's energy field auras, enters your physical body through the third eye, travels down the spine all the way to the tip of your tail bone, where the 2nd chakra is located, and is then projected out through your energy field auras where it connects with universal energy again to repeat the prana energy cycle. Now, if your internal energy is not working efficiently, the prana energy's journey through your energy channels becomes difficult. Ancient Eastern cultures refer to these energy channels as Meridians or Nadis.

The Tripple Burner channel, also known as the San Jiao Meridian or Shushumna Nadi is the messenger of Prana energy - all your other channels connect to it and receive their energy from it. The Tripple Burner is your body's most powerful energy channel because it is the only energy line that is not associated with a physical organ, which means it directly feeds your body with prana energy.

Just as the third eye governs the chakra system, when the Tripple Burner channel is functioning well all your organs work well, and vice versa. The Tripple Burner energy channel occupies the whole trunk of your body in three compartments (hence its name): The top most corresponds to energy at your windpipe and is the foundation of breath. The middle burner corresponds to the abdominal organs in the region above your belly button and is the foundation of digestion. The lower burner corresponds to your lower abdomen organs and transforms and excretes waste. These compartments are known as the Three Dantians.

Disturbed prana energy in the Tripple Burner channel can create restrictions in breathing and problems with metabolism. However, before these symptoms show, your body tells you that there is an imbalance or blockage of prana energy by presenting tiny, gristly crystals at certain points on your wrists, hands and your feet. I call these 'crystals' but they're actually not crystals, they are a buildup of uric acid and calcium deposits, and they feel like small grains of sand. By gently running a deep pressure over the crystal you can break up the blockage of energy allowing a more efficient flow. Imagine it like a river dam and you are slowly taking the dam apart.

Energy imbalances at the Tripple Burner channel shows as pain behind the corner of your eye, ringing in the ears, and unusual mood swings. The Tripple Burner channel runs from the fingernail of your ring finger, up the centre of the back of your hand and arm, behind the top of your shoulder above the shoulder blade, up the neck to behind the base of your ear, then up and around the top and front of your ear to the outer tip of your eye brow.

Every energy channel works in a pair with another energy channel. Ancients referred to this concept as 'Duality'. Unlike the other energy channels within your body that connect to physical organs, the Tripple Burner channel only connects with the Pericardium energy channel. This energy channel feeds the pericardium, which is the protecting sac that holds your heart and blood vessels in place, keeping the heart in a stable location separate from your lungs and rib cage. Without prana energy running through the Pericardium channel directly from the Tripple Burner, your heart would struggle to work efficiently. The Pericardium channel is known as 'The Guardian of the Heart' because it protects your heart from absorbing unbalanced energy from the Third Eye.

The Pericardium channel runs from the middle of your chest where a branch runs downward and inward through your diaphragm to the upper, middle, and lower tripple burners. Another branch runs across your chest, around the front of your armpit, just under the trapezius muscle, and then down the bicep side of your arm to the wrist. At the hand it crosses the middle of your palm where it splits, one part running down the middle finger to the fingernail and the other part running down the ring finger to meet the Tripple Burner channel at the fingernail. Energy imbalances at the Pericardium channel show as hot palms, the '11' wrinkle at the brow crease, and superficial skin problems such as random itches or rashes.

By regularly stroking your hands with a firm pressure on the skin, following the pathway of both the Tripple Burner and the Pericardium energy channels, you are improving your body's ability to circulate prana energy, especially at times of mental challenges and emotional disturbance.

A hand massage is a realistic and discrete way to instantly stimulate energy flow at the Tripple Burner and Pericardium channels. And it feels so good:

- Start by pushing your hands together into a prayer position, making sure your fingers are stretched to their maximum and your palms are pushing together. Hold this for a few seconds to allow the energy from each palm to radiate.
- Next, hold your left hand with the fingers of your right hand supporting the back and the thumb of your right hand resting into the middle of your left palm. Gently

but firmly squeeze the fingers and thumb in towards the centre of the palm. Take a deep inhale as you squeeze, and take a long exhale to feel the whole body relax.
- Circle the thumb on the spot in the centre of the palm for another deep inhale and exhale.
- Gently lift the thumb and fingers away and finish by fully stretching the fingers and thumb of the left hand.
- Repeat exactly the same on your right hand, with the left fingers supporting the back of your right hand and the left thumb pushing into the middle of your right palm.

These two energy channels are the 'royalty' of the body's energy matrix. By visualising energy moving through these two channels you might begin to notice visible energy 'orbs' outside of your body. These orbs are representations of your energy field and they complete the energy process from your inner world to your outer world, projecting who you are and how you feel.

Celestial Body Energy Field

We've looked at energy and how internal and external energies are constantly travelling around us and through us. Even though these energies may not be visible to your eye, and you may not be conscious of their existence, these energies do affect each one of us. The energy field, also known as aura, is a powerful shield to your physical body. It acts as a storehouse for all your repressed emotions and response reactions, both positive and negative. Other living organisms instinctively sense and react to these auras.

Ancient Eastern philosophers regard the energy field to be an illuminating net of energy that surrounds the whole external physical body as an extension of your mind. It radiates light from the corresponding chakra outward through your body structure and skin. Everything that you think or do affects the energy field. In our fast paced standard of living, your mind is constantly thinking and working, and so too are the frequencies of your aura. As such it is ever changing based on the fluctuations of your mind and body wellness.

The energy field has seven layers, each layer is related to each of the seven main chakras and to the seven colours of the rainbow. Pure and shining colours surrounding your physical body indicate good health of mind, body, and soul. Murky and dull colours reveal symptoms of emotional and vibrational frequency imbalance.

The Celestial Body Energy Field is said to mirror your third eye. It is associated with the processes of awareness, radiating approximately 2-2.5 feet away from your skin appearing as a pastel indigo colour widening out to a pearlescent shine. By being aware of the celestial body energy field you are able to calm over chaotic thoughts – your 'scattered mind', or what I call the 'naughty brain'. The ancients refer to this aura as 'the doorway to awakening' because it guides you to understand your mind, body, and soul connections giving you access to better qualities of feelings and reactions.

I cannot tell you any specific practise to do that enables you to see yours or another person's energy field, because they are difficult to see. It takes constant commitment to practise before even a short, sharp shine presents to you. But, if you soften and slightly squint your eyes while looking directly at an object, you can start to notice glimmers of orbs of colour at the corner of your eye. When I am massaging I regularly notice orbs that change colour, and I smile because I will notice the colour is representing my emotional state at that time. By being aware of and connecting to each of your energy fields you can nurture the prana energy circulation, which can have a massive impact on the efficiency of the energy's journey through your internal body.

How to connect to your celestial body energy field:

- **Positive affirmations.**
  Just like you clean your body to wash away physical dirt, you may also 'bathe' yourself in positive thoughts to wash away negative energy and allow you to focus on more optimistic ideas. Repeating positive words to yourself are believed to have this effect. A great affirmation which I like to repeat:

  "My mind is strong and capable. I move forward toward my vision with clarity and insight."

  Of course this is assuming I know what my vision is at that particular moment in time. Occasionally my celestial body energy field is dull because my mind has 'forgotten' what my vision is. If you're the same, then this affirmation is soothing:

"I trust my intuition. I am aware of every moment."

- **Visualization:**
  Imagine yourself "cleaning" your celestial body aura by rhythmically breathing in good vibrations and breathing out unwanted vibrations. Literally imagine bright light entering your body and dull light exiting, travelling far away, getting smaller and smaller as it shrinks and 'pops' into separated energy frequencies. I find this is to be soothing at bedtime.

Alastair has embraced some of these practises to connect to his third eye energy, and as a consequence now he notices when his energy is off balance before he 'goes off the rails'. With his wisdom he has the awareness, knowledge, and intelligence of making mindful judgements based on his previous experiences in order to think, respond, and react calmly. He doesn't get cross with himself, he accepts and learns from each moment with compassion. I like Alastair, and I thank him deeply for his permission to share his story with you.

"The principle of wisdom is the use of will and its associated powers of choice and self-reflection." – Maya Tiwari.

Back of Your Body: The Tripple Burner Energy Channel.

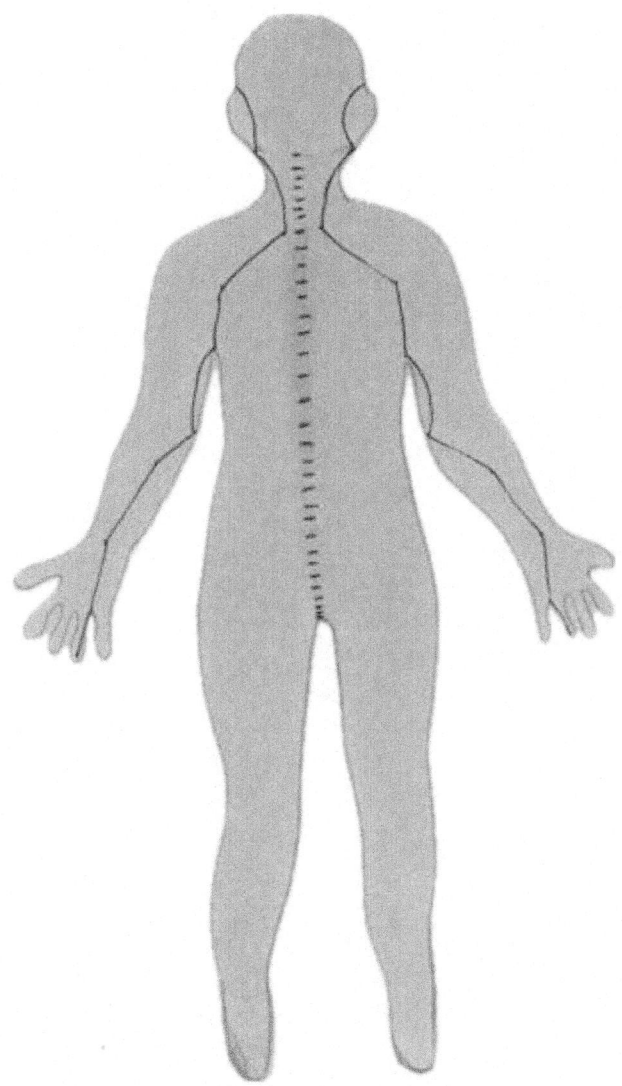

Pull tall through the crown of your head and tailbone to open the space between each 'pearl' of your vertebrae.

Front of Your Body: The Pericardium Energy Channel.

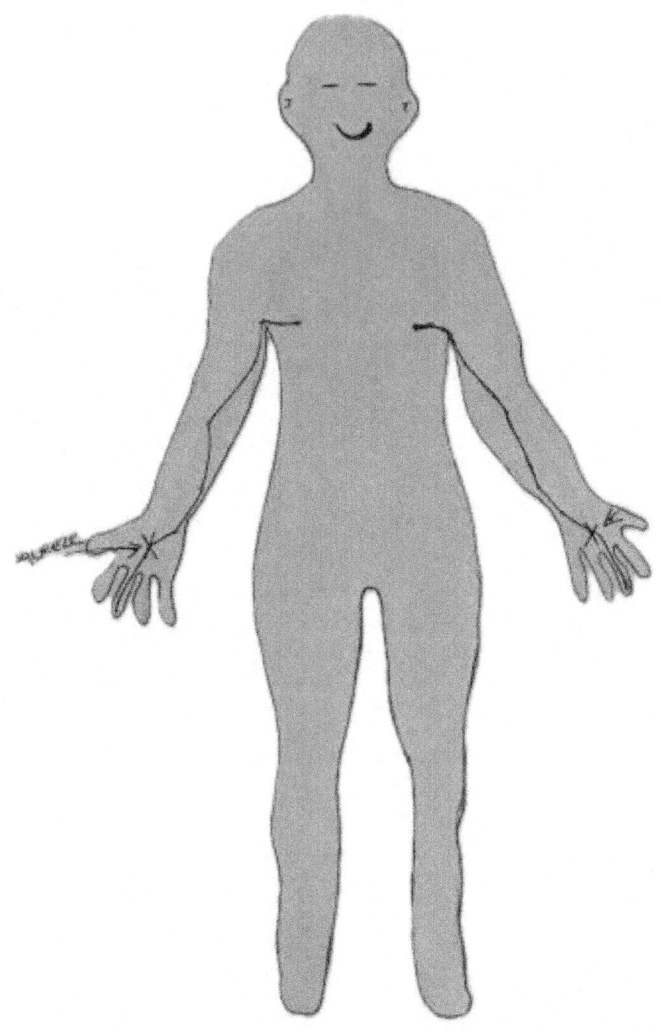

Squeeze the palm of your hands.

Ability to Self-Reflect
The Third Eye Chakra
Presents clear insight and intuition

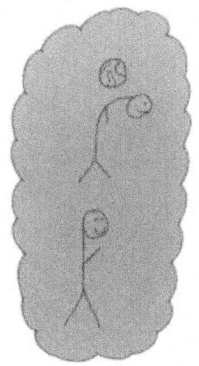

It Is About How You Observe The Bigger Picture

Do you carry the weight of the world on your shoulders?

OR

Do you accept the external stress realistically?

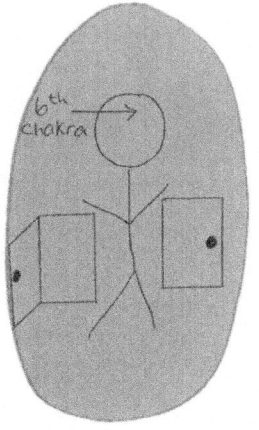

Stress Hormones

The Celestial Body Energy Field can be seen as a doorway to awakening – it is either open or closed

Pain in the corner of your eyes and the 'II' crease at your brow

Abrupt or sudden mood changes and self-doubt

Hair loss and low energy

Scents of lavender and fir

Purple colours and foods (Damson plums and dark choc)

Taking 'time out' to relax the inner chatter

Ego

Autonomic Self-Regulation
Connecting Memory to the Response Reaction

The Sacral Chakra, Oestrogen and Testosterone
Lumbar Region Energy Zone
Kidneys, Bladder, and Jing Energy
Emotional Body Energy Field

Know your own mind.
Know your own body...
and be considerate of the ego.

Autonomic Self-Regulation

Imagine your mind as a lake. Sometimes the surface is calm, sometimes the surface is disturbed. When calm you can glimpse the bottom of the lake. When disturbed, waves and ripples disrupt your ability to see the bottom of the lake. Internal and external conditions of the lake also influence the possibility to see the bottom. Think of the bottom of the lake as your inner self, or your soul. Think of the internal and external conditions as the energy systems – your outer world and your inner world.

In contemporary living we are very aware that good well-being equals balanced emotions and 'normal' levels of physical and psychological stress. We are increasingly encouraged to talk more, and do more of what makes us feel good. It is becoming more widely accepted that men and women regularly take time for self-care. And, although we cannot look into another persons' mind, there are a few indicators that show how a person is generally getting on - after all, doesn't looking good mean feeling good? But what about the inner self... are you allowing glimpses to the bottom of your lake – and are you brave enough to uncover and look deeper at how your soul interacts with the surface?

Louisa has been in my world for the majority of my adult life. We used to go out dancing together. There were six of us in our group, all 18 years old strutting our stuff in Batley Frontier Nightclub. Laughing, dancing, bumping each other into people on the dance floor to create an 'open dance space' where we welcomed everyone to "come join us!".

For years we would do this almost every weekend. Oh my, we

laughed – oh how we laughed! And oh how fabulous Louisa looked...

> √ Hair, makeup, her style, her attitude all radiating femininity.

> √ Louisa walked with grace and was amazing on the dance floor, although she would say she wasn't a good dancer she was more of a creative dancer – arms and pelvis waving and shaking about in time with the music.

> √ Louisa had, and still does have, a vibe of gentle sexuality without it being obvious or too much.

> √ Her nickname is still today Audrey (Audrey Hepburn) because she knows how to let go, to flow, to move, and to feel pleasure in everything she does, usually with healthy boundaries for herself and others, without feeling anxious or guilty of the experience.

That was until the night ended. Every time, Louisa would find herself in an argument. And then tears. Not sad tears, and not happy tears. These tears were different. The drama and tears were histrionic – excessively theatrical and totally out of the blue. Often the argument was with one of us girls over a light hearted passing comment. One example that sticks in my mind:

Louisa: "I love you."

Girls: "Awww, we know."

Louisa: "Yes but I really love you." While wrapping her outstretched arms around us all into a tight group hug.

Girls: "Ha ha ha Louisa, you are funny."

Louisa: "No! No no no no no. You don't do that. When someone tells you that they love you, you don't throw it back in their face." (stepping backwards and theatrically shouting now) "That's totally not ok. How dare you take my affection – you take take take take take, and never give it back. I'm sick of you lot. I don't even know why I call you my friends." And then sobbing confused assertive tears.

The next morning we would meet for lunch to laugh about our antics of the previous night. Of course, no one would mention the ending of the night until Louisa would say the same line every time:

Louisa: "Sorry about last night. I get hyperactive and can't focus… You know what I'm like when I'm over excited!"

It wasn't until much later in life, long after we had stopped nightclubbing and started coffchatting instead, that we started properly talking to each other. How daft it was, going on 10 years of laughing and dancing together and yet we didn't actually know much about each other. By this time I had become familiar with body energy systems, and I was becoming more interested in the chakra system. The more I got to know Louisa, the more I could clearly see her awareness and intelligence towards nurturing her own mind, body, and soul: mainly through taking time to analyse her own behaviour and why her boundaries become blurred.

Louisa recently told me, when asking permission to share her story, that she drops her boundaries with her husband Rob when they are 'in a really good place'.

"It's bonkers, Jessica. I could write the script for how the pattern unfolds. It only happens when we are in our perfect relationship phase, it's like I'm subconsciously trying to sabotage our happy relationship. I love that feeling of connection we have, and so I push for more, wanting kisses and touch all the time… all the time! And then Rob gently brushes me off, which I take as a rejection which then leads to me asking if I'm too needy, which then leads to me picking a fight and then it explodes into me defending myself for wanting to feel validated in our chemistry. It's ridiculous. I know I'm doing it, but once I'm in that zone, I can't stop it! And it only happens when things are really good." Louisa questioned herself when she said this "When things are too good?".

And then it became clear to me… Louisa's 'end of the night drama' years ago was connected to her emotional identity. When Louisa becomes over excited with energy, like having too much of a good time, the frequency at her sacral chakra cannot transform the external frequency energy quick enough and so her projected energy can become emotionally unstable. Louisa pushes boundaries, becomes extremely sensitive of being accused or blameworthy, and she gets dependent on validating her emotions.

"If I'm honest, Jessica, deep down I know the reason I'm doing it is because I am questioning why I deserve this amazing feeling of joy with Rob. That's the crux of it, I'm confused that I don't deserve our deep connection."

'Bingo' I thought!

Connecting Memory to the Response Reaction

Everything that exists is a form of energy vibrating at extremely fast frequencies. The human mind is a combination of external universal prana energy and internal 'inner self' energy bouncing off one another with an exchange of information - this we call consciousness. Going down a psychological path for a moment, consciousness can be defined as an awareness by the brain of internal and external existence. In order for your human consciousness to be in sync with other human consciousness, information has to be harmoniously exchanged.

The brain is an organ that houses many parts, and is split into two hemispheres. Its different parts serve different functions, as do its two hemispheres. The left hemisphere is associated with logic and reason, perception and focus. The right hemisphere is associated to emotion, creativity and intuition. Before information is processed by the right hemisphere, the left hemisphere takes a look at the information, filters it and tries to make sense of it. If processing of information through your energy systems becomes overwhelmed or blocked, the information can bypass the left hemisphere and the right hemisphere will accept any information that comes its way.

As we have begun to explore, human beings are a collection of millions upon millions of vibrating energy frequencies that are able to experience and express consciousness. Ancient Eastern philosophers regard this as a spider web of intimate beauty that can make up and pass right through a physical body - the colours, the designs, and the beautiful way things appear around us.

You are not a passive receiver of the information. You participate in this information, you retain this information, and you respond to this information. Ancients refer to this as

'Wisdom and Ego combining to make cognitive memory'.

- Wisdom gives you the awareness, knowledge, and intelligence of making mindful judgements based on previous experience in order to think, respond, and react calmly.

- Ego is the identification of self – the making of the 'I'. It provides your mind with a state of subjective illusion ingrained from previous experiences which have impacted cognitive memory.

Cognitive memories are the accumulation of resolved and unresolved experiences established throughout life from birth. These memories subconsciously trace every moment of your life journey, attach and stick to your energetic body systems along the way, and can unexpectedly ignite positive or negative emotions that influence your response reaction at any time.

Consider, for a random example, a person who is an activist for peace. Ordinarily you would assume they behave in a non-violent manner. Generally, wisdom is present in their demeanour and they 'think before they act'. But somewhere along their life journey they have experienced an emotional trauma that is not logically resolved within their energy makeup and that trauma has become trapped in their body energy systems. Imagine this activist for peace communicates with someone who threatens or challenges their notion of peace. The activist lashes out either physically, verbally, or both. Their unresolved cognitive memory has awakened, and their ego mind has pushed rational wisdom to a state of illusion - causing the peace activist to do and say things that can be categorised as 'out of character' for them.

These unresolved and deregulated feelings are within all of us.

They are real, and they can really mess up what we thought was a good time. Ancient Eastern scriptures and writings show these energetic dramas were happening aeons ago, as part of the human energy matrix. The scriptures and writings also show how these unresolved cognitive memories can be resolved. It takes time and commitment to the process, but these overwhelmed or underwhelmed body energies can be harmonised through the reflexes of the endocrine system, the nervous system, and awareness of the sacral chakra.

The Sacral Chakra, Oestrogen and Testosterone

Body energy is said to represent the four forms of life: mental, emotional, physical, and spiritual energy. The chakras are spinning wheels that control the internal circulation of body energy. When the frequency of internal energy, Qi and Jing, travelling through each chakra is too high or too low, the speed of the chakra's rotation changes. When you practise controlling the speed of each chakra's rotation to match its natural frequency, your body energy flows much more efficiently. This stability of internal body energy flow influences the endocrine system through the production of hormones that are controlled in the pituitary gland – the 'Master of Glands' associated with the third eye. In turn these hormones balance the information exchange within the brain allowing your mental, emotional, physical, and spiritual energy (your nervous system) to be at ease.

Simply put, for a relatively content life we need balance in these four energies, and to gain balance it is necessary to regulate the vibrational frequencies at each chakra for the body's hormones to direct the ego - the 'naughty brain'.

In this process the chakra play a crucial role in regulating and controlling mental and emotional energy - Wisdom and Ego. Having said that, we know the communication between the outer world and the inner world does not 'just happen', there is a massively coordinated dance at play, and this dance is a dual activity of masculine and feminine energy.

Interestingly, each chakra represent stereotypical male and female qualities. The odd numbered chakras 1st, 3rd, and 5th are masculine by nature and are associated to willpower and assertive characteristics. The even numbered chakras 2nd, 4th, and 6th are feminine by nature and are associated to openness and compassion. The whole chakra system is a balance of masculine and feminine energy: yin and yang.

Do you recall Louisa radiating feminine energy on the dance floor, and then later sobbing confused assertive tears? Could that be a sign of overwhelmed masculine and feminine energy?

Amazingly, all human hormones naturally function the same throughout each adult, regardless of being male or female in gender, or young or elderly in age. That is true with the exception of the Follicle-Stimulating Hormones (FSH) which control the development and growth of the ovaries and testes, and although both sexes do actually produce oestrogen, progesterone, and testosterone hormones they each function entirely differently between the sexes, undergoing particular changes at certain times in an individual's life. Also, fascinatingly, the reproductive hormones are the only natural chemical substances that are not vital to individual survival, but they are vital to our emotions and how we express ourself within appropriate social contexts.

The testes are the reproductive endocrine glands of the natural and fully grown male body, and lie in the scrotal sac. Each testis consists of approximately 200-300 lobules that secrete male sex hormones known as androgens. Testosterone is the most important androgen because it stimulates the development of the male reproductive organs, facial hair growth, Adam's apple development, a deeper voice, and muscle density. Testosterone is also produced in small amounts in a woman's ovaries to help with growth, maintenance, and repair of reproductive tissues. In both sexes testosterone is linked to feelings of reward and can influence decision making.

The ovaries are the reproductive endocrine glands of the natural female body, and they lie on the lateral walls of the pelvis, one on each side, held in place by several ligaments. Each ovary contains small masses of cells called ovarian follicles that when fully grown secrete the female hormones oestrogen and progesterone. Oestrogen is responsible for breast development, wider hips, and fatty and subcutaneous tissue development. Progesterone plays an important role in the menstrual cycle and pregnancy. Men also produce oestrogen and progesterone in the testes. In both men and women these two reproductive hormones are linked to feeling good, muscle strength and stamina, and they play a major role in what is commonly known as 'brain fog' and the processing of information.

The sacral chakra is located at the tip of your tail bone and is considered 'The Seat Of Prana Energy' because it is where internal prana energy travels to before it is projected out through your energy field auras, to repeat the prana energy cycle. The sacral chakra is the 2nd chakra in the chakra system and is very closely connected with the 1st chakra - often the two interact. The sacral chakra is also said to be the 'Dwelling Place of the Self' because it is associated to the Ego and the awareness of exploring and solving problems. The sacral chakra represents your most primitive, sometimes animalistic and deep-rooted instincts – ultimately it is what makes you who you are. Centred on personal identity, the 2nd chakra governs masculine and feminine energies. It enhances your ability to form healthy relationships, and to connect intimately with others, both emotionally and physically. In body energy healing, the sacral chakra is usually the first chakra to focus on before moving on to the root chakra, and that is why we are looking at the 2nd chakra before the 1st chakra.

Also known as the Naval Chakra and Swadhisthana, the sacral chakra is ultimately connected to desire. Uncontrolled desire can quickly turn to a longing for more. Have you ever experienced wishing for something so much that when you eventually get what you want you actually find that you're not satisfied and immediately begin wishing for something else? That is an example of a desire for more, and it also reflects an imbalance of energy between the sacral chakra and the ovaries or testes hormones.

When we have an imbalance between the sacral chakra and the ovaries or testes hormones we can also experience physical issues such as:

- hips or naval pain
- lower back discomfort
- urinary problems
- prostate or womb issues
- complications with the bladder and kidneys

Before any of these physical symptoms present, psychological emotions arise to warn us of an energy imbalance often shown as:

- fear of losing pleasurable sensations
- resistance to change
- a block in solving problems
- dissatisfaction with life
- sudden intense displays of affection
- unhealthy social boundaries
- feeling disconnected from the world
- and in extreme energy imbalance: a lack of desire and passion which can suck others' energy because of a lack of excitement and happiness

The ancient Eastern philosophers spoke of practical solutions to balance the frequencies at the chakras. The natural vibrational frequency of the sacral chakra is 417hz. When the sacral chakra is balanced at this frequency it is possible to rise above the animal instinct and become more receptive to surroundings rather than looking for something that isn't there. Remedies include surrounding yourself with the colour orange and by indulging in a gorgeous pamper – take a long bath using cedar, jasmine, or sandalwood scents, savour a delicious meal of orange coloured foods such as pumpkin, carrots, butternut squash, apricots, cheddar cheese, and sweet potatoes. Or do something logical that uses your left brain hemisphere like complete a jigsaw or crossword. Placing Golden Topaz, Citrine, or Carnelian crystals in the palm of your hand can release calming energy. The biggest healing practise at the sacral chakra is movement.. especially movement in your lumbar region.

Lumbar Region Energy Zone

The lower back, hips, and belly area is the place where we store primitive feelings and emotional reaction patterns. You know when you are consciously experiencing a special moment you can sometimes feel overly happy, and then on other occasions you can feel overly obsessive, fearful, or paranoid? Eastern philosophers regard these as 'survival patterns of past trauma creating strong primitive patterns'.

If you are able to logically solve the traumatic issue at the time, and if your body has enough strength to transform the blockage into a functioning vibration, the cognitive memory is released. But if we do not deal with the traumatic issues in the moment, if the energy gets repressed and 'shut down', the cognitive memory sticks to your energy systems like a sleeping gremlin waiting to awaken, and once awake it can cause chaos at any moment. The gremlin will show itself occasionally throughout the years, but it is thought to fully awaken 30-40 years later, wanting to be known.

Let's go back to Louisa for a moment. When Louisa was 13 years old her mother and father separated. Her mum became focused on filling her own life with pleasure, and her father disappeared off the scene. Louisa was regularly alone each evening, left to make her own meals and keep the house in order. Each weekend she would stay at friends' homes, soaking in the affection and attention her friends received from their parents as something she would one day experience. To the outside world Louisa was fine, she was a mature 13 year old able to deal with the sudden change in life. Louisa repressed, bottled, and stored her emotional trauma.

Now Louisa is in her late 40's she has started to notice her 'body feeling old'. Her physical energy is struggling with regular water infections and lower back tightness. Although she eats good food and has joined a gym, she puts it down to being exhausted and needing a good holiday. 'After a luxury break I'll be back on track.'

However, as we know, the body is amazing and it is constantly talking to us. The belly and lower back is said to be the 'Old Stuff Centre', often associated with family issues. The space between the belly button and the hip bones all the way around the back to the spine is known as the Lumbar Region. Eastern thought states any experience of unworthiness, guilt, or shame is linked to physical energy problems in the lumbar region. So it makes sense then that Louisa's lower back problems and belly aches and pains are actually manifestations of 'shut down' energy from unresolved emotional trauma.

These emotional traumas become a theme and show throughout life as deregulated emotional outbursts, frustration, and often times a belief of not deserving the good in life.

Experiences or traumas that affect the sacral chakra include:

- Inappropriate childhood conditioning
- Unacceptance
- Critical judgement
- Negative criticism
- Something, or someone, taken from us without our permission
- Violation of body or personal space, including physical touch

The lumbar region is said to be where we store our primitive feelings and where we create strong emotional patterns in response to experiences from the past. A lot of internal body energy is unconsciously focused on transforming this energy at the sacral chakra, and it can be quite exhausting on the Central Nervous System.

Your central nervous system plays a crucial role in everything you do by keeping track of both conscious actions, like moving, and unconscious actions, like waste elimination. The central nervous system is divided into three sections:

Brain: Processes information, thoughts, and memory.

Spine: Houses the spinal cord, chakras, and energy channels connecting your brain to the rest of your body.

Neurons: Carry signals to relay information from the brain through the central nervous system to the body's organs, and vice versa from the organs through the central nervous system to the brain. The information within the neurons regulate thoughts, feelings, movement, wound healing, sleep, heartbeat, response to stress, metabolism, coordination and body balance.

The central nervous system at the lumbar region assists in transmitting information to the kidneys, bladder, and ovaries or testes, and are involved in the process of eliminating metabolic waste. By practising body posture movements that open your lumbar spine, you can balance the energy at the sacral chakra and assist in regulating the survival patterns of any emotional trauma.

A great posture stretch to open the lumbar spine:

Tilt your pelvis in-line: Adjusting and lifting the weight out of your hips can help regulate your nervous system. It helps to imagine a plumbline running from the tail bone down to the floor directly between your parallel feet. As you tilt your pubic bone forward, you want to feel long through the groin area and across the front of the hips, as well as two inches taller through your waist. Do not sink into your lower back – grow tall.

Throughout my 20+ years of body movement therapy work I have seen this posture stretch almost immediately reduce lower back pain, and create a sense of self-confidence and emotional clarity. It really is incredible how being body aware can be so powerful on the emotions. And the foundation of emotional wellness is said to be based on the principle of 'letting it go'.

Kidneys, Bladder, and Jing Energy

As we know, the body contains numerous channels through which the body's energies flow. Physiological and psychological functions of the body are known to be intricately interwoven with the energy channels. Each ancient Eastern culture has its own name for these channels: Meridians, Spiritual Energy Paths, and Nadis to name a few. They're all understood the same though. In ancient Indian Sanskrit, the word 'Nadi' literally means flow or current, although in recent times the word nadi has also been translated to mean 'nerve'. Ancient Eastern texts say there are around 72,000 nadis located all over the body. I imagine them as the roads that connect the body's organs and endocrine glands to the body's roundabouts - the chakras. The nadis and the chakras operate very closely together.

To recap, prana energy is energy from the universe, sun and stars that enters the physical body through the third eye. Composed of the environmental energy that surrounds us, prana energy enters the body, travels down to the sacral chakra via the Shushumna Nadi where it exchanges information with the internal energy systems, and then ascends the Shushumna Nadi while projecting the energy back out to the environment where the prana energy cycle begins again.

Jing energy is another vital energy, but this one circulates internally. It is the life essence energy absorbed from food and water, and is essential for all life activities. Without a good supply of Jing energy living a good, long life can be difficult. Jing feeds the body's organs with metabolic energy and is used every day to pump blood, digest food, excrete waste, and enable the hormonal senses. There are three forms of Jing energy:

- Pre-natal Jing nourishes you whilst you are developing in the womb. At the moment of conception your pre-natal Jing energy determines your basic wellness for life, and at birth it is stored in the kidneys. Pre-natal Jing only moves from the kidneys when it is essentially needed, usually in highly stressful situations.
- Kidney Jing is also stored in the kidneys, however this substance moves through the body at certain times of growth and development. It plays an important role in maintaining body strength during the major phases in life such as at puberty, and a women's transition into menopause.
- Post-natal Jing is continuously circulating your body and is acquired through the metabolism of food, drink, and breathing.

Activities such as overworking, over stressing, and abusing your body will burn this life essence and consequently shorten your life span.

Of the 72,000 nadis throughout your body, there is believed to be thirteen 'gross channels', also known as body systems, such as The Digestive System and The Circulatory System. Material substances of nutrients, oxygen, hormones, and waste products circulate in these gross channels. Additionally, there are subtle channels in which frequency vibrating energy continuously circulates. The three main subtle channels are Sushumna, Ida, and Pingala in which prana energy circulates. These three channels sub-divide into fourteen subtle channels where other frequency vibrating energies including Jing energy circulates. The fourteen channels then in-turn divide into many thousands more throughout your body. These fourteen subtle channels work in pairs, Yin and Yang, creating seven groups, and these groups work in a chain of events to nourish and defend one another.

If one channel of the seven groups is out of balance, it begins to create energy blockages that obstruct your whole body energy flow. Physical and emotional signs and symptoms immediately start to show as a way to communicate to you that it needs some tender loving care.

The kidneys and bladder channels work as a pair, and they work with 'the old stuff' - old emotions that are finished with and no longer needed. They act as part of your body's purifying process that eliminates waste. Imbalances here are said to be due to opposing masculine and feminine energies within.

The Kidney energy channel feeds the purifying process and works hard to maintain a balance of opposites within your body – hot and cold, masculine and feminine, right and wrong. The kidney energy channel runs from the back of each little toe, through the outer side line of each foot to the outer heel bone where it hugs the back of each heel to the inner ankle bone and the centre sole of both feet. From there it reverses back through your inner ankle, up the inner calves, curves at the inner thigh where it ascends directly up the front of your body on both sides of the belly button to the collar bones. The Kidney energy channel controls the use of all three Jing energies and helps to purify your blood. It is closely associated with a healthy transition through each of your life stages, from early childhood through to the ageing process. Energy imbalances show as movement in your teeth, weak bones, sweating or burning soles of the feet, ankle swelling, dry tongue, and prostate or menstrual problems including unusual inflammation of your genital area.

The Bladder energy channel symbolises the release of emotion and the desire for you to let go rather than cling to the past. The bladder energy channel runs from the inner corner of each eye, joins at the crown of your head to run down the back centre line of your head where it splits at your neck to run down each side of the erector spinae to the back of your legs and knees and continues down the centre side of each calf to the outer ankle and the outer edge of each little toe. The bladder energy channel influences posture, especially in your lower back. Obstructed energy flow shows as excessive or scant urination, random headaches, lower back problems, weak ankles, sciatica, and dry skin on the lower leg and ankle area.

Each of the seven groups of subtle nadis respond to low intensity stimulation as a way to restore your body's vital energy flow. A fantastic way to give gentle stimulation to both energy channels is through a simple ankle massage, and by following the pathway of both the Kidney and Bladder energy channels you can improve your body's ability to circulate Jing energy, especially at times of emotional overwhelm.

Here's how to instantly stimulate energy flow at your Kidney and Bladder channels:

- Wrap the index finger and the thumb of your right hand around your right ankle in a 'pac man' grip (like your hand is a puppet) with your index finger just under the inner ankle bone, and your thumb just under the outer ankle bone.
- Gently squeeze your index finger and thumb in to the fleshy part of the inner and outer ankles.
- With firm pressure, pull your right hand back towards the tendon at the back of your right ankle, drawing an imaginary line to the back of the heel.
- Continue by pulling your hand off your ankle and then throw that energy away - just chuck it over your

shoulder, but make sure you're not scattering it on to someone else!
- Repeat the exact same squeeze and pull along the left ankle using your left index finger and thumb.

Kidney and bladder problems along with oestrogene, progesterone, or testosterone hormone issues and lumbar region aches and pains all tend to arise when we have difficulty letting go of emotions – particularly negative ones. These repressed emotions become trapped within our emotional body energy field and make a massive impact on our attachment to the ego.

Emotional Body Energy Field

Repeating myself just a little now, the energy field, also known as Aura, is made up of many interconnected layers, each of them corelating to a different aspect of your physical body and the way you express yourself. These layers transmit information between the seven chakras and your body's surrounding environment. Each layer has its own natural vibrating frequency, size, and colour. The layers extend outward from your physical body and change its vibrancy to match the rotating chakra's energy. Sometimes the corresponding layer may govern your body's energy chakra, and at other times the corresponding chakra is more dominant. Chakras access prana energy and transform higher vibrations in the energy fields to a lower 'workable' frequency.

The Emotional Body Energy Field is the second layer of aura and is connected to the sacral chakra. It stores feelings and emotions and is consequently known as the 'Emotional Baggage' aura. The Emotional Body Energy Field also gives the emotions strength, which is massively required when withdrawing from the ego.

Appearing as a soft cloud always in motion, the Emotional Body Energy Field circulates your physical body approximately 1-3 inches away from your skin. When you are experiencing emotional turmoil this energy field can appear like a barbwire and can grow inward to penetrate the physical body and access the ego mind. An orange aura indicates that the sacral chakra is naturally rotating at its active frequency of 417hz allowing you to fully enjoy life's pleasures. People with bright orange auras are usually creative people who are passionate about what they do; they often have a strong appreciation for art, music, or other forms of creative expression.

A cloudy, murky rainbow coloured emotional body energy field indicates imbalance at the sacral chakra and shows negative emotions are strong. This is when you notice you are excessively seeking pleasure and pushing boundaries with others. It is at this stage that you need to pay attention to your feelings of safety and security. You will greatly benefit from checking in with your ego and giving it a good telling off.

How to connect with your emotional body energy field, and tell your ego to do one:

- **Properly dancing.** By that I mean completely letting yourself go – dropping your ego and having a good time is an excellent way to cleanse emotional baggage from your emotional body energy field.

- **Visualisation.** Imagine you are surrounded by a bubble of pure orange light, where any emotions that you no longer need bounce off – they cannot penetrate you any longer.

- **Positive affirmations.** Get rid of any negative thoughts and emotions that dwell. Redirect the energy you spend on feeling insecure or in need of more emotional safety by repeating:

    "I am in the flow of feelings. I am strengthening the connection to myself."

It is important I tell you here that Louisa's story is not representative of the female gender only. I know of many men who have experienced similar. Regardless of a person's physical gender, the body's energy systems are never completely male or female. They are a combination of both. The female energy, Yin, represents acceptance and receiving. The male energy, Yang, is about doing, go-getting, and giving. Combined, they provide you with strength to manage the daily energetic changes that have been ingrained from previous experiences and their relationship with the ego.

"Just as the breath of the blue sky is calm, so the will of those who are pure will be in peace and the breath of the orange earth will be stable. Those who fail to preserve this harmony will find protection is lost. This is said to injure one's own body and to destroy one's own life essence." – Huang Ti Nei Ching Su Wen.

Back of Your Body: The Bladder Energy Channel.

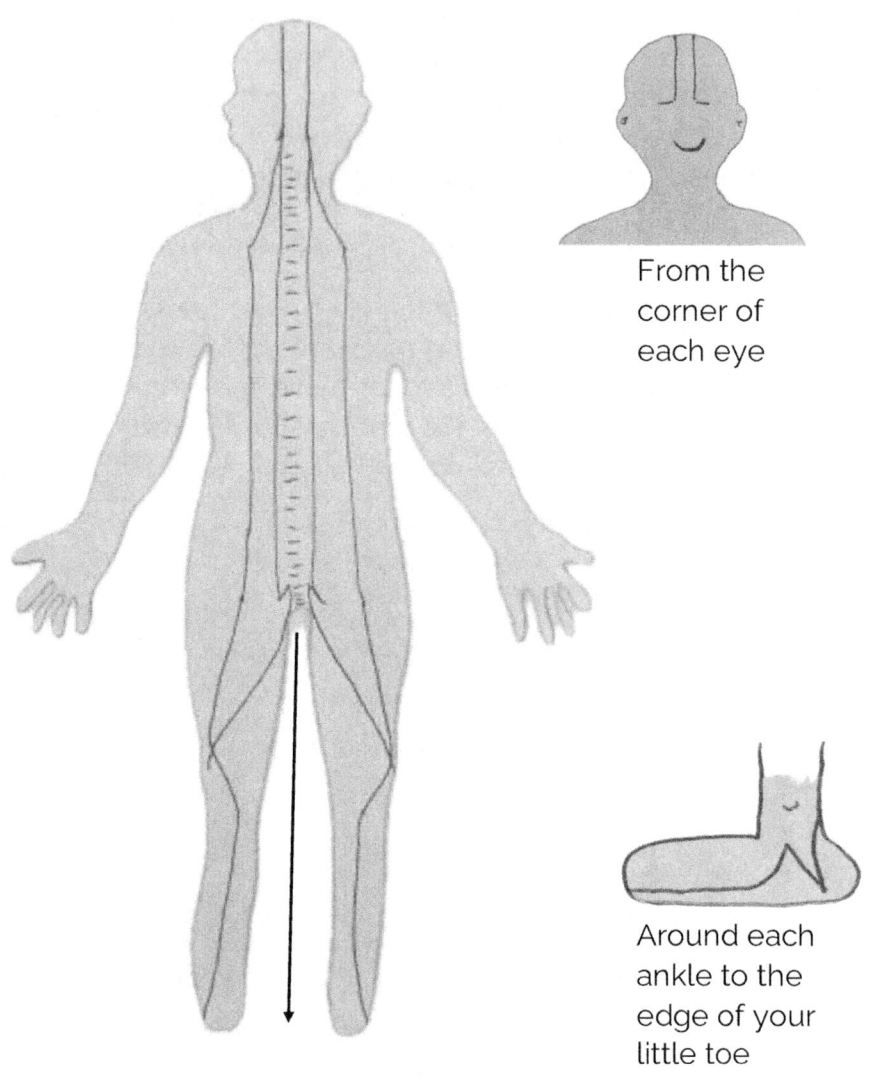

From the corner of each eye

Around each ankle to the edge of your little toe

Tilt your tail bone in line with your feet

Front of Your Body: The Kidneys Energy Channel.

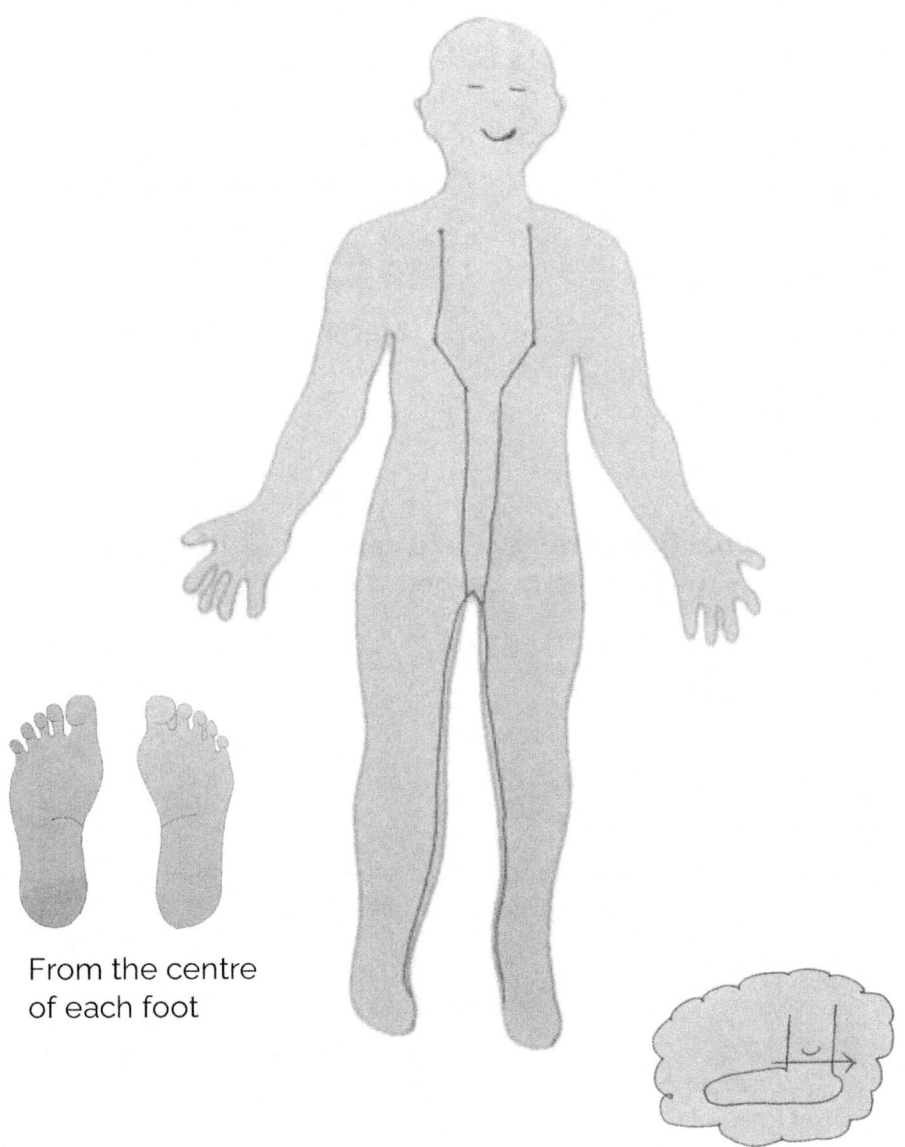

From the centre
of each foot

Squeeze and pull under the ankle bones towards your heel

Feeling Safe and Secure
The Sacral Chakra
Connected to the Ego

It Is About How You Express Yourself With Emotional Clarity

Are you a pussy cat

OR

Are you a lion?

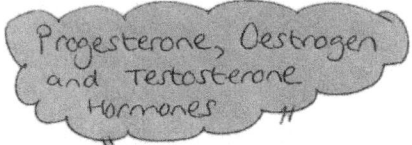

Masculine & Feminine

The Emotional Body Energy Field can be seen as a fluffy cloud or barbed wire

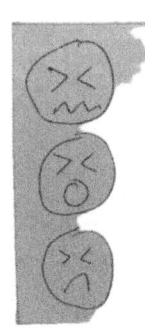

Lower back, belly, and hips discomfort

Intense displays of affection. A desire for more

Teeth movement, ankle swelling, and burning feet

Scents of cedar or jasmine

Orange colours and foods (cheddar cheese)

Logical thinking like crosswords or jigsaw puzzles
Dancing with complete freedom

Unity

The Role of Perception With The Ego and Wisdom
The Whole Wellness

The Root Chakra and the Adrenal Glands
Pelvis Region Energy Zone
Stomach, Spleen, and Qi Energy
Etheric Body Energy Field

Everything is vibration.
One who understands this understands everything
is different rates and realms of experience.

The Role of Perception With The Ego and Wisdom

The ears, the skin, the eyes, the tongue, and the nose are the five sense organs we use to perceive, acknowledge, and make a judgement on the external world. With the help of these five sense organs directly, not only do we notice the external world, we also develop our understanding of our existence within it. More than that, we absorb every detail into the body in the form of energy. This is known as Direct Perception, and in ancient Eastern traditions the concept holds significance for understanding another person's inner world before judging their outer world. Traditional Chinese Medicine and Ayurvedic Medicine both recognise the importance of establishing sense connections.

Direct Perception is based on acquiring knowledge of a situation as a result of the sense organs, the mind, the body, and the soul connecting as one - we do not just perceive situations physically, we also connect to a situation psychologically and emotionally. To perceive a situation is to sense, to feel, to comprehend, and to know. But our perception can be tainted by our own feelings according to our childhood conditioning, education, or social values. It seldom happens that two people perceive a situation in the same way. Problems can be due to our own perception of events rather than to what actually happened. If there is a weakness in any of the sense organs, if the mind is not calm, and the soul is not stable then complete knowledge of a situation cannot be gained. Expectation is then created and a judgement is made.

The Dalai Lama wisely says "Expect nothing, and you shall not be disappointed." I love this. In our fast paced, noisy world where anticipation of a situation often leads to disappointment, this teaching reminds me to be more mindful and wise, to release my attachment to outcomes and to make decisions aligned with long-term wellness. But then again, that takes bravery, self-confidence, and actually a deep sense of stability, security, and connection to the physical world. And what if I don't always feel that way?

We have all at some point been overcome by feelings of hopelessness, fear, greed – all the deep seated emotions based on security and safety when experiencing uncomfortable situations. Difficulties can derive from a poor ability to accept or the need to reject what we perceive. We can even deny or close off from a situation completely. This is the ego. The ego remembers, evaluates, plans, and responds to the outer world. It influences our perception by putting up defence mechanisms to protect our inner world from anxiety and distress.

The best outcome then would be for the ego to interact with wisdom. To make balanced decisions considering both inner world reactions and outer world consequences with empathy, compassion, and a broader perspective of our own right to exist in this moment. Easier said than done though, isn't it.

The root chakra, the first chakra in the chakra system, is our prominent energy wheel for direct perception It gives us a feeling of having the right to be here, and the right to have. It is connected to our sense of belonging. When our sense organs along with mind, body, and soul vibrations are balanced we meet challenges with acceptance:

- √ we feel grounded or 'rooted'
- √ we trust the world, within reason
- √ we feel optimistic and motivated
- √ we offer safety and support to others

√ our place in this world appears valid

Conversely, when there is imbalance at the root chakra, there is a strong fear of not belonging. When two bodies vibrate with unbalanced energies at their root chakras, they cannot possibly exist in balance together. Try and try again, if both people have weakness in the root chakra then perceptions of experience become blurred, expectations rise, and judgment can become deeply unkind.

The Whole Wellness

During the end of the 2020 – 2022 Covid period a good friend of mine, Karen, needed to fill in the money gap and so she took on an extra job as Office PA for a family-run company. She loved that job. She felt comfortable and secure there where everyone was friendly and supported each other. Karen's fun and outgoing personality along with her strong 'can do' attitude suited that role perfectly.

Eric was the company Managing Director. Karen and Eric would speak regularly each morning. From the get go Karen and Eric's work relationship was honest. They had a good vibe together. A few months into her new job Eric offered Karen a promotion. More money, company pension, and maybe the opportunity for a company car. Karen couldn't believe it.

Karen: "It just seems too good to be true."

Me: "When do you start your new role?"

Karen: "I don't know, we didn't talk about that. I was so excited I forgot to ask!"

Three weeks later Karen was still working as Office PA. Eric encouraged Karen that "Yes, hopefully the promotion is yours."

Another six weeks later and Karen was still the Office PA. Eric would now pass by without speaking. Occasionally he would nod his head in acknowledgment, but rarely would he smile. She worked extra hard trying to please Eric, but he would be difficult and often she felt her completed work wasn't good enough.

She expected better of Eric "Well, his careless attitude is just a clear indication of his arrogance." Karen's confidence at work dwindled. Feelings of self-doubt and low self-esteem raged through her. She was often late for work, her sciatica had flared up, and she regularly forgot to do simple tasks. She was treading on eggshells - being aware of everything she thought, said, and did.

"I feel like I'm on a rollercoaster. I constantly feel sick when I'm at work now. And I don't even know what has happened!"

So with that in mind, let's take a look from Eric's perspective. He employed Karen who was bohemian, independently strong, and fun. He was aware that the company needed her energy and in a bid to keep Karen in the company, with knowledge that Karen was struggling financially, Eric wanted to impress Karen by discussing the potential of a promotion with her. He needed time to structure the promotion and so he left it a few weeks before he next mentioned it to Karen. Six weeks passed and Eric realised the business couldn't sustain a promotion for Karen just yet. He felt overwhelming anxiety that Karen would assume he had failed her. He withdrew from any communication with her in embarrassment.

Karen's rapid decline in her work ethic disappointed Eric. He didn't expect her to be so contrary with her lack of interest and sulking. He did not want the stress, and he certainly did not need the addition of irritable bowel that the situation had brought. He was aware his resistance to speak with Karen created tension in the whole office, but he refused to change his attitude of "The promotion idea wasn't official. She can resign if she wants to."

Two very different perspectives to the same situation. Both Eric and Karen experienced a lack of safety and security, and as such they both perceived the situation from their ego mind. When ego is active, the brain is not able to explore solutions to problems that might easily be thought of when wisdom is in play. This problem was due to Eric's and Karen's own individual ego perception where there was a weakness in their ability to see the situation for what it really was - neither mind was calm and their souls were not happy. In an attempt to self-protect, expectation was directed towards each other and critical judgement was made. This scenario could be played over and over again in many different situations and between many different relationships. Ultimately though, the end result would be the same. When we are not certain of what we are experiencing we push the process into the arena of conclusions. This occurs when a person's sense of knowledge around the situation is so weak that the naughty mind perceives everything inaccurately.

The wisdom of the ancient Indus Valley of India, the teachings from the Vedas, advise to 'Never jump to a conclusion or make unrealistic expectations, for conclusions and expectations provide poor judgments, and the root chakra becomes wounded.'

The Root Chakra and the Adrenal Glands

The Root Chakra represents survival instincts, stability, self-defence, material and financial security, self-protection, and greed. It allows you to stay centred and present in the moment.

When you face responsibilities or situations you struggle to manage or control, it is natural for you to respond with a little bit of tension. You recognise the feeling: your heart beats faster, you feel heavier in your chest, muscles across your neck, back and shoulders are tighter, your breath shortens, your head hurts, your eyes squint, you feel a lump in your throat, your hands shake, butterflies are in your tummy. This acute stress can be motivating in certain situations.

But if the situation becomes a struggle or you are unable to manage or control the pressure, you want to cry, your skin condition changes, your bowels become irritated, you can't switch off, your mood becomes low, you realise you are living in dread of the 'what if', if sleep occurs at all your dreams are anxious, you are close to burnout. This chronic stress is not helpful.

Stress can be defined as any state of tension caused by a difficult situation. Effects of stress are associated with the Adrenocorticothrophic Hormones (ACTH) that stimulate and control the adrenal cortex, the fight or flight mechanism, and are generally 'rooted' in feelings of anxiety or fear about basic survival needs such as money, shelter, food, belongingness and love.

When a stressful or dangerous event occurs the external information is transported to the amygdala, which are two almond shaped clusters located just behind the pituitary gland, one in each hemisphere of the brain. The amygdala is the powerhouse of emotional information. It is a key player for linking the root chakra to the sacral chakra with the emotions of reward or fear, and the resulting emotions of pleasure or frustration. The amygdala is incredible because it interprets external sensory stimuli, processes the information, values the moment, and turns it all into cognitive memory.

If the interpreted information is perceived as a threat, the amygdala sends the information to the pituitary gland which then immediately sends signals to the adrenal medulla endocrine glands for the release of adrenaline into the blood stream. This is when we get the sudden cold sweat, sharpened senses, an increase in mental and physical power, and a 'natural high' that can last minutes or hours. Sometimes when we are already on edge we can experience an 'Amygdala Hijack'. This is when the amygdala overreacts by perceiving a little occurrence as a huge threat – like when someone casually walks into a room and you jump a mile "Ohhhh you made me jump!", and then you physically shake for a short while after. Some people can become addicted to the 'adrenaline rush' from the amygdala hijack and seek out opportunities.

As the root chakra is all about your sense of safety and security, so too are the adrenal glands. They are small triangular shaped endocrine glands, each one sits on top of each kidney, underneath the ribcage on each side of the spine. The adrenal glands secrete essential hormones that help regulate your metabolism, immune system, blood pressure, and response to stress.

The adrenal glands are composed of two parts:

> **Adrenal Cortex:** This is the outer part of the adrenal gland. The principle hormone secreted by the adrenal cortex is cortisol – the main stress hormone that

regulates the body's stress response.

The adrenal cortex also links to the sacral chakra (2nd chakra) by producing testosterone, oestrogen, and progesterone hormones.

Adrenal Medulla: This is the inner part of the adrenal gland. The principle hormone secreted by the adrenal medulla is adrenaline which prepares the body for 'fright, fight, or flight' response via the central nervous system.

The adrenal glands and the root chakra work in partnership together, and when their energies are balanced:

√ the body feels grounded and comfortable

√ the mind is at ease and the body moves, feels, and looks at ease

√ we experience a sense of trust in the world and feel safe and secure in our everyday lives

√ feelings of uneasiness or threat dissipate relatively easily, and instead we feel connected to our own source of support without a need to rely on another person to provide that support

The root chakra is the first of the seven, and is the foundation of the entire chakra system. Ancient Eastern scripture's definition of the root chakra translates to 'root support'. It is believed that if the root chakra's rotation is restricted then the other chakras in the body are affected. Located at the very base of the spine, it is closely connected to the sacral chakra (the second chakra), and the two often work in tandem with each other. Also known as the Base Chakra, and the Mooladhara, the root chakra is situated between the genitals and the anus at the perinium. Your body relies on the root chakra for connection to yourself and others around you.

The root chakra is aligned to basic survival needs. When rotating at a natural frequency of 396hz it brings us emotional strength in the face of fear and anxiety, and also brings us a feeling of security - which often goes hand in hand with an aura of strong physical presence. The root chakra partners the adrenal glands and the excretory system which includes the kidneys, skin, lungs, and intestines to remove waste from the body.

When the body and mind are nourished, energy flows to the root chakra. But when there is imbalance of energy at the root chakra, which can be either over energised or underactive energies, information is not accurately interpreted and signals from the brain are immediately sent to the adrenal medulla at the adrenal glands to over release adrenaline. Signs and symptoms of irregular adrenaline secretion include:

- unexplained weight gain or weight loss
- digestive issues at the stomach and spleen
- frequent body weakness
- skin condition change
- weakened immunity including fatigue and feeling run down
- frequent sickness or illness including nausea
- unbalanced blood pressure

Psychological emotions arise to warn us of an energy imbalance, often shown as:

- insecurity, irritability, and obsessiveness with safety in 'basic needs' of money, shelter, food, belongingness and love

- uncontrollable feelings of being ungrounded – a fear of "Rocking the boat"
- a fear of rejection
- low self-esteem, lack of confidence, and self-doubt
- irrational stress about money and financial security
- a feeling of instability, insecurity, and fear of being stuck in life

In addition to psychological emotions, problems with whole body wellness show, such as:

- issues with the pelvic floor muscle
- aches and pains in the pubic area, tailbone, or tops of the thighs
- sharp pains in the feet
- difficulty sleeping
- appendicitis
- an increase in excretory processes such as rapid breathing, increased sweating, tense muscles, dry mouth, frequency of urination, and a feeling of nausea in the stomach

The root chakra is powerful and can affect all of the other chakras. The ancient Eastern philosophers spoke of practical solutions to balance the frequencies at the chakras. Ironically, given that adrenaline produces a short-lived rush of immediate power to the mind and body, power does activate the root chakra. Eating a nutritious meal with red coloured foods such as beetroot, apples, skinned tomatoes and peppers, hot spices, and kidney beans can provide the physical body with prolonged powerful energy. Try envisioning the colour red glowing at the base of the spine, grounding you to the earth. Scents of cassia, clove, and nutmeg helps you feel present, focused, and dynamic in this moment. Placing smoky quartz, ruby, onyx, garnet, or hematite crystals in the palm of your hand can release calming energy to the root chakra. The biggest healing practise for the root chakra though is reconnecting with your body – posture and breath work can be massively beneficial.

Pelvis Region Energy Zone

The attitudes you hold towards yourself, your family, and your ability to survive are all shown in the way you move - the posture of your spine, the way you place your feet, and the way you hold your pelvis. It is at your tailbone and pelvis where emotional stress is stored, and ancient Eastern philosophers say that stress in the pelvis, such as sciatica, deep lower back aches, constipation and even appendicitis, are all to do with trust and fear of the future, a resistance to what is happening, a build-up of irritable emotions, or an inability to admit what you are really feeling.

As you know, stress activates the automatic release of adrenaline. Approximately 20 minutes after the release of adrenaline, cortisol is released. Cortisol helps to mediate the stress response, regulates the metabolism, maintains immune function, and reduces inflammation. It is not such common knowledge, though, that regular and long-term release of cortisol can cause the pituitary gland at the third eye to 'pause' production of cortisol, leading to continual tiredness, nausea, weight changes, and inherently lower back and pelvis pain. These physical issues are due to muscular stress in the pelvic floor muscle. The pelvic floor muscle is the powerhouse of the lower Dantian area. It is similar to a hammock in how it connects the back of the tailbone to the front of the pubic bone, allowing for the prime support of all the organs in the pelvis. Don't confuse a stressed pelvic floor muscle as a weak pelvic floor muscle. A stressed pelvic floor muscle simply means the muscle cannot engage fully, meaning a tight or overactive pelvic floor muscle can be just as stressed as an underdeveloped or weak pelvic floor.

One of the most powerful ways of reducing stress in the pelvic floor muscle is by engaging the 'Tilt Your Pelvis In-Line' posture correction (from the Lumbar Region Energy Zone chapter) and the 'Pull Tall Through The Crown Of Your Head' posture correction (from the Cervical Region Energy Zone chapter) when standing and walking. This means lifting weight out of your pelvis by pulling tall through your tailbone and crown of the head while tilting your pelvis inline to feel long through the front of your hips.

Ancient yogis advise to practise 'Pelvic Floor Engagement' ('Vajroli Mudra' for men, and 'Sahajoli Mudra' for women) so that when the stressful times do come, you are enabling the pelvic floor muscle to support energy flow through the chakra system, helping to strengthen your ability to stand your ground and to feel safe and rooted in the world.

Simple to do:

- Start by sitting or standing comfortable with the pelvis in line and lengthening tall through the spine, while breathing naturally. Remember to look forward rather than down.
- On your next exhale draw your urethra upward. This is the action when squeezing in a wee. The testes in men and the labia in women should contract slightly upward during this squeeze.
- Once you feel confident that you are contracting the urethra upward (not pushing down), try engaging the anus. On your next exhale draw your sphincter upward, as though you are holding in wind.

As an important side note here, it is not healthy to hold urine or wind in. To quote my mum "Better out than in." This likeness is just to give an example of the correct physical feeling.

Releasing stored emotional stress from the pelvis is essential for the entire trinity of mind, body, and soul wellbeing. Ancient

Eastern philosophers say unusual aches and pains in the pelvis and pubic area can be related to:

- a lack of financial support
- a lack of emotional support
- a betrayal by someone we trust, including oneself
- a rejection or abandonment – especially in childhood
- overly critical judgements made by others
- survival from incidents related to accidents, abuse, violence, or neglect

The practise of deep rhythmic Ujjayi breathwork while engaging the pelvic floor mudra is a fantastic way to get the emotional release of insecurity and fear, and increases feelings of presence and self-awareness:

- Sit comfortable with your mouth and jaw relaxed,
- Inhale a deep breath to your belly button. If this is unfamiliar try putting a hand on your belly button and feel it rise as you breathe in. Don't worry if this feels odd at first, it is our natural way to breathe so just focus on the waist expanding and you'll get it.
- Exhale the sound "Haaaaaahh" as though you are sighing.
- Now close your mouth and breathe in to your belly button through your nose. Push your tongue into the roof of your mouth.
- Make the same "Haaaaaahh" sound as you exhale through your nose.
- Once you have got the sound on the exhale, try making the "Aaaaaahh" sound on the inhale.

The breath should sound like the tides of water, or a gentle snore coming directly from a baby's belly.

Ujjayi breathing encourages the free flow of Jing energy and Qi energy throughout the whole chakra system, energy channels, organs, and energy fields which ultimately provides a gentle vibe of being calm and grounded.

Stomach, Spleen, and Qi Energy

All living things are changing constantly. Thoughts and emotions are changing. All our dreams, fears, wants, and wishes are constantly changing. By realising that emotions are temporary you can gain a more direct perspective. The more you recognise that everything is in a constant flow of change, the more you can notice life is only an ebb and flow of yin and yang energy.

Yin and Yang depend upon each other – one cannot exist without the other. They transform and control each other. When one becomes dominant it has a tendency to weaken the other.

Yang energy is known as masculine energy. It is recognised through:

- Active and assertive confidence in speaking up, and is achieved through structure, logical thinking, and taking charge.

Yin energy is known as feminine energy. It is noticed as:

- Compassionate and reflective intuition with gentle forgiveness, and is achieved through creativity, slowing down and being present 'in the moment'.

Qi is the body's internal life force energy that holds the structure strong against the pull of gravity. All vital functions in your body are governed by the movement of Qi. Without Qi your organs would be heavy, your skin would hang down, and your body systems would work very slowly. It travels through all energy channels around your body and is stimulated through movement and action. In ancient Chinese culture, Qi is said to be the body's innate intelligence that influences the internal environment to create overall balanced wellness. It's flow is understood as an invisible force similar to the lymphatic system due to the cycle having no beginning and no end. It travels through every part of the body's energy channels and lasts 24 hours after which it replenishes and repeats. Weakness in the mind, body, or soul can throw this pattern off kilter, depositing more energy than required in some areas and causing deficiency in other areas. This creates energy imbalance in the chakras, energy channels, and energy fields resulting in feelings of illness as opposed to wellness.

When you get stressed your nervous system goes into fight or flight mode, tapping into the adrenal glands to release adrenaline. If cortisol is not released efficiently enough, the flow of Qi is disrupted and can become stagnant, resulting in your whole body feeling swollen and stiff.

Now, remember that Jing is the body's essence for energy. We are born with a prenatal Jing which is stored in the kidneys and is only released during illness, injury, or emotional trauma healing. Post-natal Jing is acquired through metabolising food and drink and is nourished with exercise. Jing feeds the body with energy and is used every day to breathe, pump blood, digest food, excrete waste, and enable the senses. When Jing flows well, we are in control of our senses, and therefore the adrenal glands function well.

Qi is yang. Jing is yin. The two must be balanced for them to work together and generate your internal electricity. Without the flow of Qi and Jing there would be no life. A quote from The Yellow Emperor's Classic of Internal Medicine comes to mind here "Where there is free flow, no pain. Where there is pain, no flow."

Qi is stored in the spleen and gets regenerated every 24 hour cycle from post-natal Jing energy via the stomach. The spleen is said to be the 'worry house' and is believed to govern thought. The spleen is the partner of the stomach, which is where old or stagnant thoughts are held. Over thinking or excessive worry weakens the spleen, causing weakened Qi circulation resulting in restricted stomach function and slow post-natal Jing flow.

The root chakra is connected to the Spleen and the Stomach energy channels. All three together play a vital role in the wellness of mind, body and soul.

The Spleen Energy Channel runs from the tip of your big toe along the inner arch of the inner foot. From there it runs in a diagonal line to the inner ankle and up the centre line of the inner lower legs to the inner side of each knee, across the front of each thigh then up to the pelvis. It continues up the torso to the ribs and the front of the shoulder joints, where it then swoops down and around to finish just under each armpit. The spleen energy channel assists in cleansing the blood and aids the immune system by controlling body temperature. Imbalanced energy in the spleen energy channel shows as: irrational irritability, depression, uncontrolled weight change, nausea, extreme fatigue, bunions, underarm swelling, and patches of dark eczema on the skin surface.

The Stomach Energy Channel runs from underneath each eye, down between each side of the nose and cheek to each corner of the mouth, where it then runs to the outer edge of the jaw line up to just above the temple in-line with the end of the eyebrow. From there it runs down to the centre of each side of the neck, descends to the front of the torso through the centre of each nipple, then diagonally to the base of each side of the rib cage, and straight down to the pelvis. There it diagonally runs to the outer hip, down the outer thigh, outer knee, outer calf to the centre top of each ankle and ends at the second toe. The Stomach energy channel assists in the 'rotting and ripening' of foods and fluids and controls descending Qi energy. Stressed or knotted Qi in the stomach channel materialises as corns, nail fungus, pelvis and thigh pains, poor sleep, dry throat issues, eye shadows, and teeth grinding.

The hands have specific points that are energetically connected to specific body organs. Just at the base of the V of the left thumb and index finger is the pressure point for the spleen. Named 'The Hand of the Valley', reflexologists and acupressure workers believe a squeeze of this pressure point can instantly stimulate energy flow at your stomach and spleen energy channels and therefore balance energy at the root chakra. It is said to relieve stress and tension headache from overthinking, and can relieve constipation and the associated pelvis region aches and pains. Here's how to 'squeeze' the Hand of the Valley Pressure Point:

- With a pincer grip of your right thumb and index finger (as though you are picking up a tiny bit of fluff), place the top pad of your index finger at the front and the top pad of your thumb at the back of the 'V' between your left thumb and index finger.
- Squeeze the right thumb and index finger with an 'in and down' push into the squishy cushion of the V. Don't worry about hurting yourself, the more you squeeze with care the better the trapped energy can release.
- Hold the squeeze for 4-5 seconds and then gently release your right hand away.

This energy release can be quite powerful and can sometimes

lead to a lightheaded sensation, so make sure you are not operating anything deemed unsafe when you perform this squeeze. As you squeeze the Hand of the Valley pressure point, take a deep Ujjayi breath in and slowly exhale to feel the stress melt and the colour from the inner body radiate outwards.

Etheric Body Energy Field

You know everything around you and inside you is what it is because of vibrating energies, and consequently the colours of your energy fields, also known as auras, are constantly shifting and changing depending on how well the external and internal energies can form a complete and harmonious whole. This is unity.

Known as Linga Sarira in Sanskrit, the Etheric Body Energy Field is regarded as the blueprint of your past and present mind, body, and soul energies. It is believed to unite your soul with your physical body, and operates as a medium for reincarnation when you die, taking all past and present imprinted memories and experiences into your next life.

The Etheric Body Energy Field is intimately connected to the root chakra – what affects the prana energy flow through the etheric body energy field affects the Qi flow through the root chakra, and vice versa. Whenever either of these two energy systems become unbalanced, it can cause negative effects on the 'harmonious whole', resulting in high stress levels, low self-esteem, and chaotic colours of the physical body's surrounding aura.

A bright peach-red aura indicates there is balanced energy radiating from the etheric body energy field. The mind, body and soul are united, as are the energies of wisdom and ego. Disturbed or blocked energy emitting from the etheric body energy field shows as a fire red aura. A dull brown fire red aura usually means a person is over analysing and often over thinking situations. They are too heavy in their thoughts, which is dangerous territory for making critical judgements and unfair conclusions. A dull orange fire red aura shows a person is needing to be in control - their vibrational frequencies are expressing a need to lead. They appear fearless in many ways and as such come across as bossy or domineering. Similarly, this is dangerous territory for making critical judgements and unfair conclusions.

By trying to be present in the moment, present with yourself, and present with the world around you, your etheric body energy field and root chakra have an opportunity to connect in harmony, allowing uncomfortable situations to pass with ease and therefore avoiding anxiety and distress.

Here are some other great ways to practise uniting the root chakra and the etheric body energy field:

- **Positive affirmations:** Feel rooted in the world by repeating "I am here and I am real". This self-talk can also quickly re-establish your connection to direct perception, especially when you find yourself in a difficult situation.

- **Connecting with the earth**: Walking barefoot helps energy flow to the root chakra. Grounding allows you to be energetically connected to the earth through the legs and the feet, and feeling secure in the legs and the feet allows a positive reinforcement of moving forward in life. If outdoor barefoot walking isn't practical for you, move about the home barefoot. It can help to improve your body awareness, which ultimately can help with the release of muscle stress, especially at the pelvis region.

And, of course, breathe. As simple as it is, a deep, full belly breath lets the mind take a moment, allows the body to relax, and gives the soul a chance to feel safe and secure.

"Before anything, first regulate your breathing on which your temper will be softened and your spirit calmed. For when that is under control, the earth will be at peace." – Baha'u'llah (the founder of the Baha'l'Faith).

Front of Your Body: The Spleen Energy Channel.

Ujjayi breathing

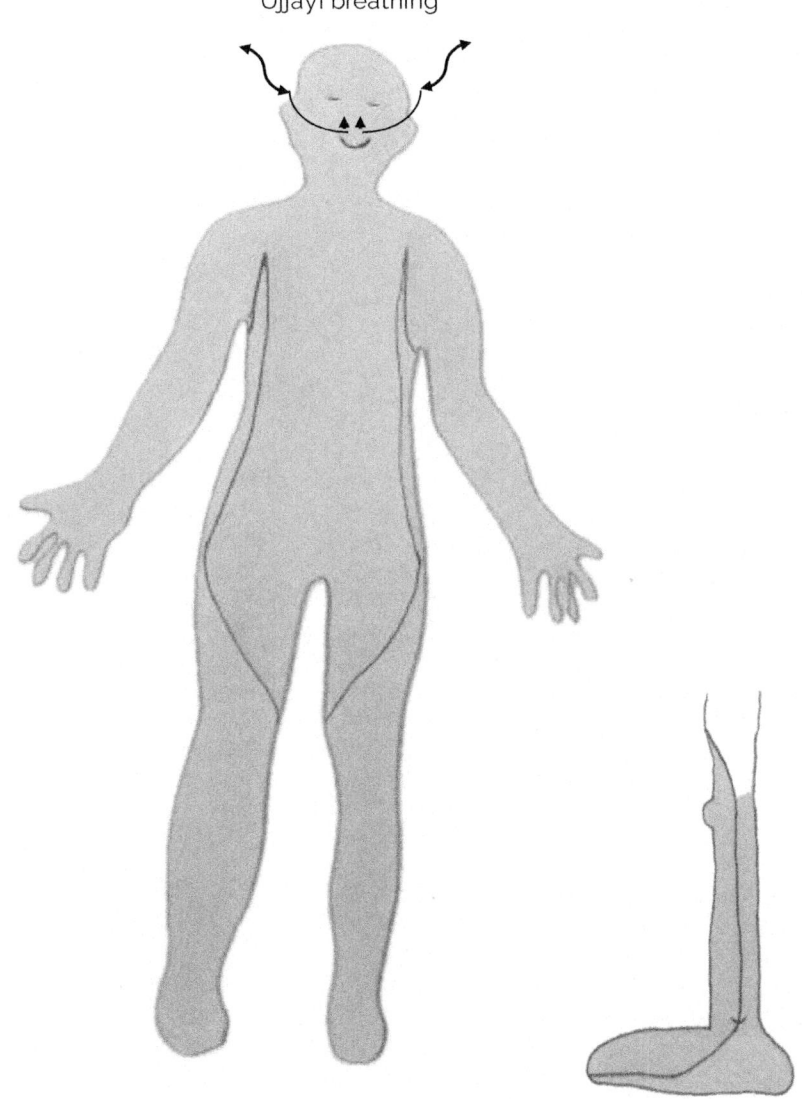

From the tip of your big toe up your inner leg

Breathe through your nose making a sound like tides of water

Front of Your Body: The Stomach Energy Channel.

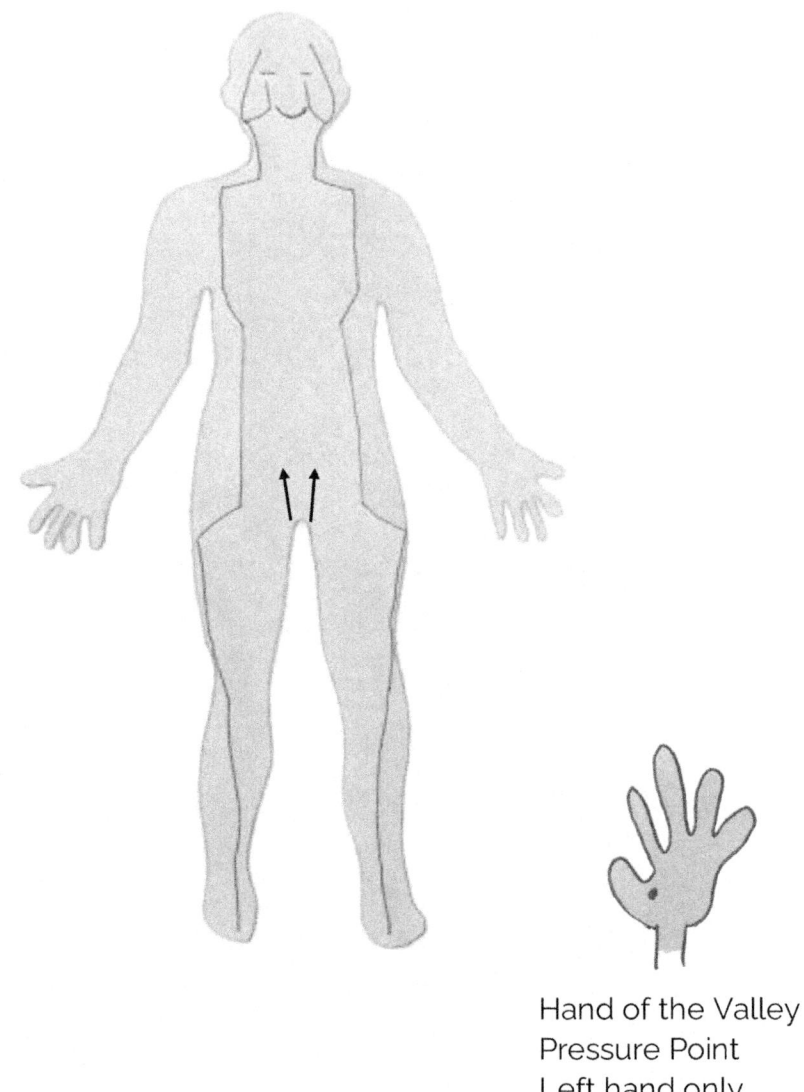

Hand of the Valley
Pressure Point
Left hand only

Engage your pelvic floor muscles by pulling your urethra upward. This is the action when squeezing in a wee

Feeling Strong and Grounded
The Root Chakra
Your survival instincts, sense of belonging, and self-protection

It Is About How You Manage Your Emotions

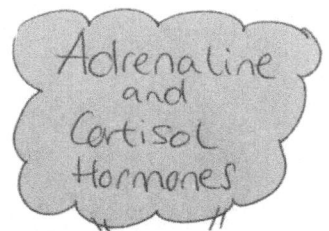

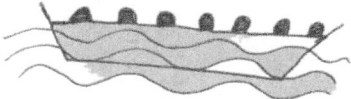

Are you afraid of 'rocking the boat'?

The Worry House

The Etheric Body Energy Field can be seen as a bubble of peach red or fire red colour

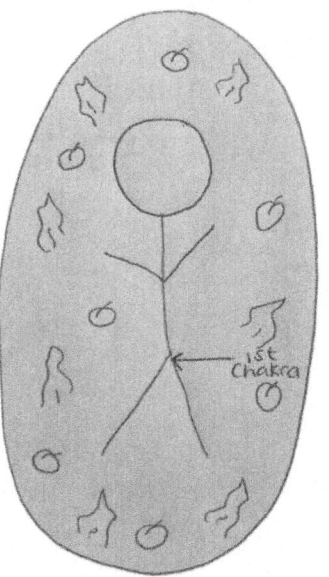

Deep lower back and groin discomfort

Extreme tiredness but you can't switch off

Eye shadows
Callused feet or bunions

Scents of cassia, clove or nutmeg

Red colours or food (beetroot and red apples)

Breathwork, posture stretches, and barefoot

Power

The Polar Energies
A Critical Part of the Body's Nervous System

The Pancreatic Glands and the Solar Plexus Chakra
Lower Leg Energy Zone
Heart and Small Intestine Channels
Mental Body Energy Field

Do things and think thoughts that
allow you to be in a state of ease.
You have the power to control your vibration
rather than your vibration controlling you.

The Polar Energies

Understanding how to direct energy can dictate the version of reality you end up with: "When we focus unattached attention on our life experiences, we are eventually able to manifest the desired result." When I first heard that statement from the yogic monk I sat with in Dharamsala, I thought "Hmmmm, not sure about that one." But actually, I now get it. If we really dislike something we will attract more negative events from it. Likewise, if we intensely love something we will attract more passionate events from it – and not necessarily a positive passion.

For example, imagine you are at a crossroads in life and you're focusing on what you do not want the outcome to be, then you are attracting the energy that reflects this negative attitude in future experiences. Similarly, imagine if you focus your attention on the outcome being amazing and everything working out perfectly, then the super charged unrealistic energy will ironically attract more challenging situations in future experiences.

Every time you feel stuck in life, when you feel you are taking two steps forward and one step back, or similar situations keep coming up in your life, it is thought to be because your body's energy field is stuck. A Chinese proverb says "Where attention goes, energy flows. Where attention dwells, energy spells". Meaning that life is only concerned with what we are focusing more attention on. And there are two main types of attention: Polar and Non-Polar.

- **Polar attention** is emotionally charged, directed towards a specific thought or outcome, and has a strong energy flow towards the two poles of our experience – extreme positivity and extreme negativity. As a result, situations that confirm past trauma keep coming up.

- **Non-polar attention** is balanced and unattached – it is a neutral observation to an experience that acknowledges and accepts change without excessive emotional response, resulting in a naturally peaceful version of reality.

If you look at a situation with non-polar attention, where you accept the present moment without focus on a specific outcome but rather as a more beneficial process, then you can overcome the challenging period with a balanced perspective and become stronger as a result. In this case you are potentially attracting a reality that reflects hidden lessons, or blessings. It is in this space of acceptance that your left brain hemisphere and your right brain hemisphere work together, allowing the version of reality to become clearer, and the energy to flow freely - revealing itself as 'the best' outcome.

Interestingly, the fundamental link between the left brain's ability to focus attention wisely and the right brain's ability to create a solution is in your gut brain - the solar plexus to be exact. The solar plexus gets its name because it has two bundles of intertwined nerve branches that look like the sun's rays radiating throughout your abdominal region. It is located directly in the V of your ribcage, behind your stomach and in front of your main blood vessel, the aorta, just below the diaphragm.

The function of the solar plexus is to control the organs within the abdominal cavity (the middle dantian) and keep them functioning efficiently. When your gut is healthy and fed well, both physically and psychologically, messages sent throughout the solar plexus to the main abdominal organs can have a positive influence on your nervous system, creating a deep sense of personal power and ultimately the ability to manifest desired outcomes to a situation.

A Critical Part of the Body's Nervous System

The solar plexus houses the Enteric Nervous System (ENS) which is like a mini brain that communicates with the Central Nervous System through many nerve cells of the gastrointestinal tract (the GI tract). The GI tract is the hollow passageway of your digestive system that leads from your mouth, around your abdominal area, all the way down to your anus. The Enteric Nervous System co-ordinates digestion through peristalsis, the contracting wave like movements that push the contents of your GI tract down through the entire trunk of your body. It is an intrinsic part of your body's digestive system for achieving adequate nutrient absorption in the gut.

The two nerve bundles of the solar plexus have five important roles within your nervous system:

- Receiving and transmitting sensory impulses in your gut area
- Initiating your fight or flight response
- Increasing hormone secretion
- Assisting with your digestive movements
- Constricting blood vessels and redirecting the blood to your muscles

Ancient Eastern cultures realised the importance of the GI tract and dedicated a large part of their life practise to cleansing and maintaining good abdominal health. It is believed that specific digestive cleansing techniques, such as Shatkarma Dhauti in Ayurveda and Nutritional Therapy in Chinese Medicine, transform the GI tract from being purely a food processing pathway into the source of living a more creative, fuller life.

As part of my Holistic Therapy service I often visit the

backstage area of arenas and theatres, providing body massage to touring musicians and artists. An international pop star, who will go by the initials P.S. requested me as his massage therapist several times while he was on tour in the North of England. He was struggling with an old, repeating injury in his lower leg. On our first meeting, I quickly noticed he was eager to speak, almost like a therapy session. I didn't speak, I didn't need to. He wasn't interested to hear my voice:

P.S: "As much as what I have achieved and experienced is glorious, it has also been the onset of mental illness for me because it is just too much. I do have good support, you know, honest people around me... It is still a relationship where I am the boss though." Short pause in talking. "Touring is not what you think it is. Outside the tour bus the other night, there were that many girls banging on the window asking for autographs. I ended up opening the window and telling them to [expletive]. They have zero understanding. It wasn't very nice of those fans". A longer pause here. "I'm clean now, but I was, like, a raging alcoholic. I was just covering up all my insecurities, sadness, and vulnerabilities with drinking and drinking and drinking. I remember I was rehearsing for a tour in Germany and I would go back to the hotel, drink a bottle of vodka and just cry. That's probably why my digestion is so messed up."

Me: "Huhhhh."

P.S: "I've said an awful lot of bad things about the guys in the band. I mean, I remember we were on tour and we'd arranged to meet up to have a chat, and then a couple of hours before the meeting I texted to say I'm not coming. I was scared that I'd go, say what I wanted to say, and then other people would say 'No, that didn't happen." You know?

Me: "Mmmmm."

P.S: "Instinctively, I know I am a loner person."

I remember thinking "Wow... why does he continue to be a 'pop star' if it is such a massive, negative experience!?"

It was later that evening, after I had thought for a while of P.S's hyperactivity and scattered talk, that I realised the textbook projections from his solar plexus chakra. He was:

√ competitive and sometimes arrogant

√ often not reliable and lacked following through on a promise (even a promise to himself)

√ low in energy and self-esteem

√ easily manipulated by others around him

√ struggling with poor digestion and abdominal cramps

√ rude and often used the victim mentality to make himself feel better

√ showing an inability to relax or switch off

Activating a healthy Enteric Nervous System is like activating your body's inherent healing energy. We all know how to eat, and we all know how to maintain our physical body in a state of health by eating only the right foods, in only the correct quantity, at only the correct time. But few people actually understand that the human body has the power to heal itself through the communication between the solar plexus, the digestive gastrointestinal tract, and multi coloured foods.

The next time I saw P.S, I gently introduced a conversation about 'natural rainbow foods' – eating coloured foods associated with each energetic chakra: red, orange, yellow, green, blue, indigo, and violet. Do you know, he absolutely surprised me. He was sincerely interested to learn more. He understood that his attitude towards his life was broken (he said this, not me), and he confessed that he really wanted to change his 'egoic' outlook – he should be grateful and proud of the life he has created (again, he said this not me). I deeply felt his change was coming, and I keep noticing it to this day as I watch from afar, as a kind fan.

The Solar Plexus Chakra and the Pancreatic Gland

Within the solar plexus nerve bundles resides the solar plexus energy chakra. Balanced frequencies at the solar plexus chakra are projected from you as having energetic vitality and being genuinely joyful and satisfied with life. This chakra is all about power and the right to act honestly while realistically going after ambitions and being transformational in life. When vibrational frequencies align with the solar plexus chakra frequency you experience characteristics such as:

√ being confident, motivated, and empowered

√ having a clear sense of purpose and direction in life

√ feelings of being lost or at a crossroads dissipate. You can make decisions with ease and clarity, feeling in control of your destiny.

Good nutrition maintains the efficient working of your body. This is common knowledge. Poor nutrition can have a dramatic effect on your general health, energy levels, sleep patterns, and stress response. This is also common knowledge. But before you even consider your good or not so good nutrition habits, have you thought about your Human Growth Hormones (HGH) and Insulin Like Growth Factor 1 (IGF-1)?

Your body relies on the chemical processes of HGH and IGF-1 to promote, control, and maintain healthy body structure and metabolism, including healthy blood sugar levels. Metabolism is quite simply the chemical processes of turning the food you eat into energy. These chemical processes go on continuously and involuntarily inside your body in order to maintain proper energy to keep your body organs functioning, your muscles moving, your lungs breathing, your tissues and cells repairing, and your liver transforming and storing excess carbohydrates, proteins, and fats. High metabolism means your body naturally needs more energy in a state of rest than someone with a low metabolism. And vice versa.

HGH is regularly released by your pituitary gland throughout every 24 hour day to stimulate growth within your body. If human growth hormones are continuously released in excess your bones can thicken, your organs can enlarge, and you become at risk of high blood pressure and type 2 diabetes. If the release of human growth hormones are restricted you carry more organ body fat, your heart can weaken, your muscles and bones can weaken and you become at risk of heart failure. IGF-1 is released by your liver to regulate and balance the levels of HGH in your blood stream, keeping your body functioning well. However, human growth hormone (HGH) can be over stimulated when there are low levels of sugar in the blood (hypoglycaemia), or restricted due to high levels of sugar in the blood (hyperglycaemia).

I'll say that again, but this time less medical... blood sugar levels, human growth hormones, and insulin like growth factor 1 hormones are controlled by your pancreas and pancreatic gland, located behind your stomach and in front of your spine. As food is digested, your pancreatic gland responds by releasing hormones into your blood stream that balance and circulate blood sugar to all muscles and tissues for immediate use. Between meals, blood sugar levels steadily decrease and so your pancreatic gland releases other hormones that communicate with your liver, nervous system and pituitary gland in your brain. Here is what happens:

When you eat, the carbohydrates, proteins, and fats are broken down by mechanical digestion of peristalsis in your gastrointestinal tract, and chemical digestion of bile, pancreatic juice, and digestive juices from your abdominal organs. Each of these processes allows carbohydrates to absorb as glucose (sugar) into your blood stream to then transport to your liver. The liver removes excess glucose from your blood, converts it into glycogen, and stores the glycogen for emergencies when Jing energy is low. As the carbohydrates are digested, your pancreatic gland releases the hormone insulin to assist in maintaining healthy levels of sugar in your blood. Between meals, when blood sugar levels decrease, your pancreatic gland stops releasing insulin and instead secretes the hormone glucagon which tells the liver to convert the stored glycogen back to glucose (sugar). Glucose is then released from the liver and transported in your bloodstream to continue feeding your muscles and tissues until your next meal. While your liver is doing this job human growth hormones are released from the pituitary gland and insulin like growth factor 1 hormones release from the liver, mirroring the exact same process. All this combined is optimal functioning metabolism.

But, and this is a big but, if your body is already energetically unbalanced, especially at your solar plexus chakra, the liver can have a hard time converting the excess glucose to glycogen, resulting in continual high levels of sugar remaining in your blood stream. Now, not only are your energy levels affected with sudden surges of hyper energy followed by a sudden energy crash, but the pancreatic gland and its hormones insulin and glucagon get incredibly confused. Insulin is now constantly required to lower blood sugar levels and consequently glucagon is not required at all. That means there is an excess of glycogen that cannot be stored in the liver and so it travels to your body's organs to be stored as 'toxic' visceral fat. With the high levels of blood sugar now circulating your muscles and tissues your human growth hormones become over stimulated, making you at risk of Type 2 Diabetes

If this process is prolonged, eventually the pancreatic gland reacts and rebels by completely stopping the release of insulin altogether. Similarly, insulin growth factor 1 hormone levels lower dramatically. You can now imagine the complete metabolic chaos in your body's energy levels then! The central nervous system neurons now kick in by sending signals to your solar plexus nerve bundle in your abdominal region, overstimulating the energy vibrations in your solar plexus chakra. Signs of unbalanced energy in the solar plexus chakra include:

- A lack of self confidence
- Nervousness
- Lack of ambition or motivation to pursue goals
- Feeling powerless to change

The Solar Plexus Chakra, also known as the 3rd chakra, Naval chakra, Manipura, and 'City of Jewels' is considered to be the most powerful chakra in relation to Jing energy and metabolism. It is regarded as the centre of your personal power and is an essential component of your whole energetic system. When your body is nourished with balanced energy the solar plexus chakra shines at a frequency of 528hz, creating what I call a 'Shen Shine'.

Unbalanced energy that effects the solar plexus chakra includes:

- Negative self-talk that reinforces limiting beliefs and undermines self-confidence and self-esteem
- Listening to criticism from others that can erode self-confidence and weaken your sense of personal power
- Lack of exercise can lead to stagnation of energy at the solar plexus chakra
- Stress takes a toll on the body and mind, leading to imbalance at the pituitary and pancreatic glands

- Eating a diet that is high in processed foods, alcohol, and carbohydrates (sugar) leads to metabolic disfunction

We can recognise negative energy at the solar plexus chakra with physical signs such as:

- Digestive issues, including eating problems
- Stomach ulcers
- Diabetes – Type 1 from childhood, Type 2 in adulthood, or Pregnancy Diabetes in the third trimester
- Issues in the liver or pancreas
- Chronic fatigue
- Stress (adrenal issues).

But before physical signs arise, emotional signs show such as:

- Unnecessary nerves
- Lack of confidence
- Frustration
- Feelings of powerlessness
- You may also experience unnecessary anger, frustration, and aggressiveness.

In addition to low physical and emotional energy, mental symptoms begin to show including:

- Lack of motivation
- Difficulty making decisions
- Feeling stuck or experiencing a lack of direction and purpose in life
- Unable to set boundaries or stand up for yourself
- Overly dominating and controlling of situations.
- Stubbornness and mental meltdowns in daily life

The purpose of the solar plexus chakra is to transform and hone in on the ability to express intensions with honesty. Joy nourishes this chakra. When any of the symptoms begins to appear it is wise to listen and respond before the signs start to show. Spend some time assessing short-term goals and long-term aspirations, laugh off flaws, and try to not take things so seriously. Ancient Eastern philosophers spoke of practical solutions to balance the frequencies at the solar plexus chakra by eating clean yellow foods that support digestion such as whole grains, basmati rice, quinoa, ginger and turmeric, lemons and avocados. All these foods help stimulate the liver to cleanse and rid the body of toxins. Scents of bergamot, lime, and grapefruit help you feel courageous with a clear determination to positively succeed. Placing sunstone, yellow citrine, or aventurine quartz in the palm of your hand can release positive energy to the solar plexus chakra. The biggest and simplest healing practise for the solar plexus chakra though is by visualising a bright yellow light radiating from your naval area (in-line with your belly button and in the middle of the V shape between your ribs below your diaphragm) filling your entire body with joyful energy. Breathe in and exhale as you feel the warmth radiating your abdominal region.

Lower Leg Energy Zone

The Solar Plexus chakra is known as the City of Jewels because it is the chakra that balances feelings of joy. It is easy to confuse joy and happiness as the same emotion, but actually they are totally different. Joy is the deep internal goose bump sensations you feel in your gut, and happiness is a psychological or physical reflection of external influences.

Ancient Eastern philosophy states that psychological issues are linked to physical problems and therefore the way we move mirrors our feelings. The legs speak out very loud. Known as the second heart, the lower legs reflect your position in a relationship - often the relationship with the self. Lower leg aches and pains are manifestations of 'want' feelings and represent insecurity or feelings of being unsure of your place in the world.

Heavy and overly strong or tight lower legs reflect an inability to be spontaneous and show you are holding onto something too tightly, possibly fearful of change. Soft and over relaxed lower legs reflect a loss of direction and being 'up in the clouds' too often. Taking time to focus on what you want is not selfish. Work out what you want to happen in the next 6-months, within reason and of course realistically, and find a clear direction of how you will make that happen – if you are consistent with the emotional commitment, I bet any lower leg pains or discomfort that you might have will begin to heal.

Movement is also very effective in relieving aches and pains in the lower legs, especially gentle movements focusing on lifting and stretching the calf and ankle muscles. Here are a few gentle daily movements that you could try:

Pada Hastasana (Forward Bend) – From standing or sitting, with both legs as straight as possible, gently bend your body forward from your lower back. Make sure your shoulders stay down away from your ears. Aim to touch your belly onto your thighs (don't worry of this is way off, just aim for it). Reach your hands towards your feet and rest your head down towards your legs. Breathe deeply, especially focusing on relaxing the lower back and keeping your legs as straight as possible. Once you feel comfortable in this stretch, gently lift your head to look forward. To release this stretch gently walk your hands along your legs towards your hips to come back to upright position. Take a moment to let your body adjust to being upright again.

Pada Sanchalanasana (Cycling) – Start lying on your back, using a cushion or rolled towel to support your lower back if needed. Pull your right foot towards your bottom so you are gently and steadily bending your right leg. Bring your right knee as close as possible to your chest. On an exhale slowly and gently straighten your right leg to take your right foot above your hip, toes toward the ceiling. Do not push this stretch through the back of your right leg, just allow the weight to relax as you lengthen the leg muscles. Inhale to hold the stretch, and on the next exhale gently bend your right leg and then lower it down to the floor next to the left leg, in the starting position. Practise the right leg five times, focusing on lengthening the middle spine while stretching the leg. Repeat on the left side five times.

Sumeru (Downward Dog) – On your hands and knees in a table top shape, make sure your hands are under your shoulders. Tuck your toes under and lift your bum up to the ceiling with your legs as straight as possible and your shoulders staying over your wrists. Take a deep breath in whilst looking just above your belly button (your solar plexus). Stay in the shape for as long as possible while breathing deeply. To release out of this shape gently bend your knees back to table top position and take a moment to let your body adjust before moving upright or to standing again.

It is up to you to decide which movement is best suited to your body, although a combination of all three movements is great! Daily practise of these movements will gain immediate relief from unusual lower leg aches and pains, and after a week or so when the stagnant energy begins to shift, surprising results can be noticed.

In addition to stretching, don't underestimate the power of talking to yourself. It is more common for people to have regular internal dialogue, but as crazy as some people might think it is, talking out loud to yourself can help you to better understand the world around you. Ask yourself simple questions like:

- "What has moved you today?"
- "What made you laugh today?"
- "What has brought you joy today?"

And then start asking deeper questions. Like:

- "What is happening in your world?"
- "Do you feel supported?"
- "Would you rather be moving in a different direction?"

Always answer your own questions out loud... outwardly spoken self-talk can help you make decisions more easily, and can also motivate you to do what you keep putting off. Maintaining a positive outlook while talking kindly to yourself can have massive impacts on your whole self-esteem, especially your heartfelt self.

Heart and Small Intestine Channels

All living things are made up of feminine yin and masculine yang. I'm repeating myself here. Qi is life force holding the body strong against the pull of gravity generated through movement and action. Jing is the body's essence for energy acquired through metabolising food and drink. The cycle of Jing is similar to the digestive system in that it transports energy to organs and tissues in a sequence. The cycle of Qi is similar to the cardiovascular system in that it transports energy to all areas of the body along the body's energy channels. Body weakness throws both cycles off kilter, depositing more yin or yang energy than required in certain areas and creating blockages in other areas, resulting in whole body energy imbalance.

Humans are made of organs that are uncannily shaped and arranged to do jobs in partnership with other organs. A perfect Yin and Yang partnership. Yin energy goes from the feet to the torso out to the fingertips. Yang energy goes from the fingertips to the face down to the feet. You know when someone's yin and yang are balanced because they radiate a 'Shen Shine'.

So if Qi is action in life (mind), and Jing is life essence (body), then Shen is life vigour (soul). In Eastern philosophy 'Shen' is the basic power of presence – the 'light in the eyes'. Shen is associated with consciousness, and the capacity for your mind to form balanced ideas and your body to live life to its full. You cannot have a 'Shen Shine' if you do not have balanced Qi and Jing.

Shen is known as 'The Heart's Mind' because it resides in the heart energy channel and is believed to be the true essence of the mind. Different activities such as connecting with nature, connecting with others, and connecting with ideas or philosophies that make you feel alive and inspired illuminates your Shen Shine.

The solar plexus chakra is connected to the heart energy channel and the small intestine energy channel. Both play a vital role in the distribution network for prana energy. Prana is the collective life energy that holds your body, mind, and soul together. You obtain prana from the atmosphere and it travels through the chakra system before projecting outward back into the environment as speech, action, behaviour and perceptions. The heart energy channel encourages movement of prana energy upwards through the chakra system, and the small intestine energy channel encourages movement of prana downwards. Wellness of the entire mind, body, and soul trinity determines how much prana we can transform in the body to radiate a Shen Shine.

Another way of looking at Shen is to think of those whose energy is contagious, those individuals who have power and influence to move groups of people towards a common goal. If you want to be powerful, you need your Shen to shine. When someone has balanced Shen they easily flow with nature and universal rhythms, they feel plenty of joy. When someone has imbalanced Shen, they experience uncontrollable emotions like sadness or unhappiness. You can build up your Shen without too much effort, and it all comes from aligning the energies at your heart and small intestine energy channels.

The heart energy channel originates in your armpit and runs down the internal side of the whole arm to the inner wrist, where it continues down the metatarsal of the little finger up to the V of the little finger and ring finger. From there it wraps over the top to the front and ascends up to the inner base of the little finger nail. Symptoms of requiring stimulation within your heart energy channel are: a lack of depth when interacting with others, irrational thoughts, forgetfulness, insomnia, lower leg pains, and sweating more than usual,

The small intestine energy channel originates from the outer side of your small finger down to the wrist and continues to the inner elbow and swoops then to the outer elbow. From there it runs diagonally to the back of the armpit. It continues up to the back of the shoulder where it continues along the collar bone in a zig zag line to the centre of the neck, then it runs in another diagonal line to the centre side neck, jaw, base of cheekbone and up to the ear. It controls the digestive fire and the transformation of solid to liquid food processing. It also sorts through thoughts and ideas. Symptoms of requiring stimulation in the small intestine energy channel show as a lack of joy, self-deprecation, pessimism, poor leg circulation, hot tongue, swollen throat, earache, and stiffness and pain in the shoulders.

When we are experiencing heartache or emotional stress we tend to have an upset gastrointestinal tract – constriction in the throat, pain in the abdomen, and a change in waste elimination. This prolonged emotional upheaval weakens Shen and begins to physically present itself through slouched posture, dullness in the eyes, and heavy movements. Remember, the heart energy channel houses the mind and is in charge of our mental health. The small intestine energy channel separates chaotic thoughts from clear thoughts. When there is dysfunction in the small intestine energy channel there is also dysfunction in the heart energy channel. Same goes the other way round. Joy and a true appreciation of life depends on the ability of the small intestine and the heart energy channels working as one.

Appreciation of life can be found when going back to basics and learning how to properly breathe a simple 'belly breath'.

Practising belly breathing is essential to your well-being, and by practising properly you are giving yourself time to settle your mind and your body, and therefore your soul becomes settled. Because belly breathing brings about a deep inner calm it is necessary to approach it consciously and with awareness.

The practise is simple:

- Begin by exaggerating your inhale slightly by deliberately pushing out your abdominal area.
- Then exhale slowly while being aware of the breath leaving the abdominal area and travelling your upper body. Extend your exhale so that it lasts two or three times longer than your inhale. For example breathe in for a count of 3 seconds and extend your exhale to last between 6 and 9 seconds.

Too often we begin breathing exercises with a tendency to inhale into the upper chest area, lifting the shoulders up toward the ears while focussing on short breaths into the nostrils. But guess what… it is best to ignore the nostrils completely at this stage, and focus your attention on the movement at your solar plexus!

- While concentrating on filling the solar plexus area with breath you are allowing the belly cavity to rise and fall, to expand and contract. Once you feel this connection with ease in the V of your ribcage, then begin to concentrate on the sound of the incoming breath and not the action of breathing itself. Practise Ujjayi breathing where the sound of your breath is similar to an ocean wave, or a baby snoring. This sound will pull the breath along a full 3 second counted inhale. Then exhale for 6 seconds while concentrating on the sound of the breath leaving the body and travelling slowly, very slowly, upward and outward, opening wider to fill the space around your head and shoulders.

As you practice the solar plexus breathing take note of your shoulders becoming looser, your head feeling freer, and your subtle smile stimulating a moment of inner joy. Surrender and allow the bright energy to radiate throughout your diaphragm area, across your ribs to the front and back, feeling warm, secure, and strong.

Mental Body Energy Field

Since time immemorial commentaries on the energy systems have been shared. Traditional Eastern cultures still today verbally pass teachings through the generations as 'life lessons'. The principle of ancient teachings is based on 'everything moves, everything vibrates, and everything is surrounded by an energy field.'

The overall size of the energy field is influenced by physical, emotional, and mental wellness. When you stand strong in your personal power the energetic connections throughout your body are constantly flowing. You experience a positive outlook without fear of taking risks, and you venture into uncertainty with balanced hope and courage.

The mental body energy field is the third layer of aura and is connected to the solar plexus chakra. It is associated to the rational world and the functions of thought. It radiates outward approximately 3-8 inches away from the physical body as yellow orbs around the shoulders and head that brighten when balanced energy is engaged, or cloud over with imbalanced energies.

People with bright yellow aura are decision makers with a strong ability to analyse with detail and close discrimination. This energy field is all about having appropriate reactions and as such are drawn towards numbers, data, and navigation – anything that requires a penchant for meticulous analysis and discriminating attention.

It is believed this mental body energy field is the vehicle of thought vibration and enables the manifestation of the self. Healing at this energy field is stronger and longer lasting than the other body energy fields, but it needs to be approached from a holistic view encompassing ideas, thoughts and behaviours as well as clean eating and loving kindness. It is within your mental body energy field that your truths and perceptions are formed, and often determines whether you remain stuck in life or you propel forward. The saying "Raindrops keep falling on my head" comes to mind.

Your mental body energy field serves as a filter between your mental awareness and the patterns you adopt during your life. An unaware mind results in too much mental chatter, or noise, that keeps you stuck in negative scenarios, dulling your Shen Shine and making you unable to distinguish between what is really needed and what is not. Feelings can get locked in the mental body energy field and manifest as an obsessive attitude with a feeling of being right all the time while emotionally longing for something more.

Developing awareness of your mental body energy field is the basis of achieving a balanced mind, and the best way to create a glowing Shen Shine is by starting with the food you eat.

- **'Brain foods'** – Clean foods and drinks make a massive difference to lifting the weight from your mental focus and your overall mood. Cut down on the processed sugar and simple carbohydrates. Try adding more yellow foods to your daily diet like walnuts, lemons, turmeric, egg yolk, whole grain cereal, squash, corn, and (my favourite) homemade soda bread. Bananas are great, but be careful because they have a high starch content which is difficult to digest and can be a factor in rapid weight gain.

- **Positive affirmations:** Gentle self-talk can powerfully encourage your mind to release the patterns that you want to change. Regularly tell yourself: "My power is growing every day. I can, and I will."

- **Reassess your 'wants':** Sorting through your 'to do' list, or even creating a realistic list of what you want to achieve with non-polar attention can give a fantastic boost to your vigour and adventure for life. Remember, it is also good to ask others for support in making your dreams happen – you can't do it all on your own and still have a bright Shen shine!

Ultimately though, the energy associated to the solar plexus chakra and the mental body energy field requires balance – a balance of power and love. Realising that it is ok to say no to others and to say yes to your own wants is not always selfish. Finding a balance in the ability to both give and receive joy can be the awakening to living life well.

"Anytime we can listen to true self and give the care it requires, we do it not only for ourselves but for the many others whose lives we touch." – Parker Palmer

Back of Your Body: The Small Intestine Energy Channel.

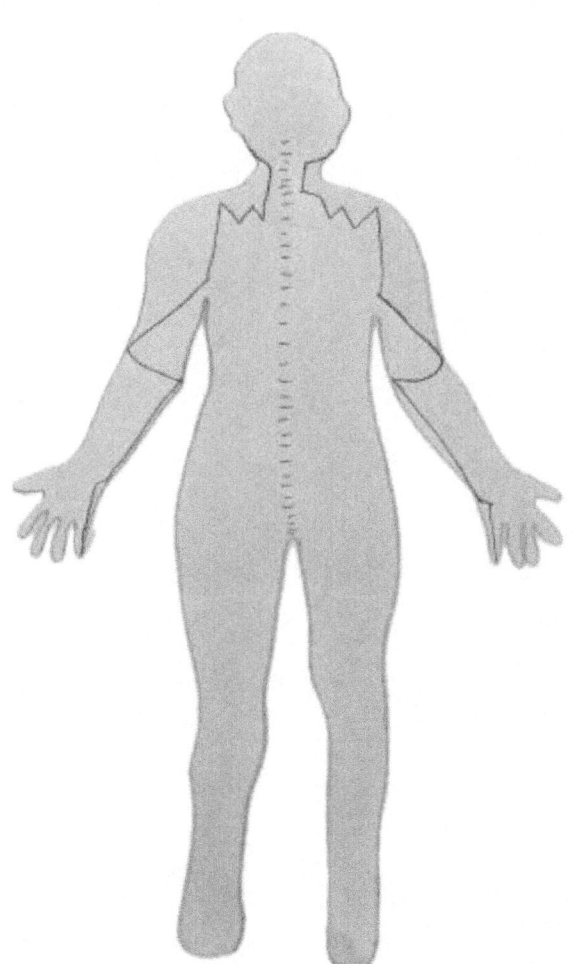

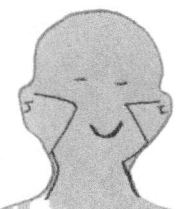

Up to your cheek bones and outer ear

Lifting and stretching your lower legs helps to relieve aching calves and ankles

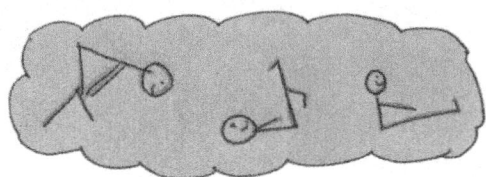

Front of Your Body: The Heart Energy Channel.

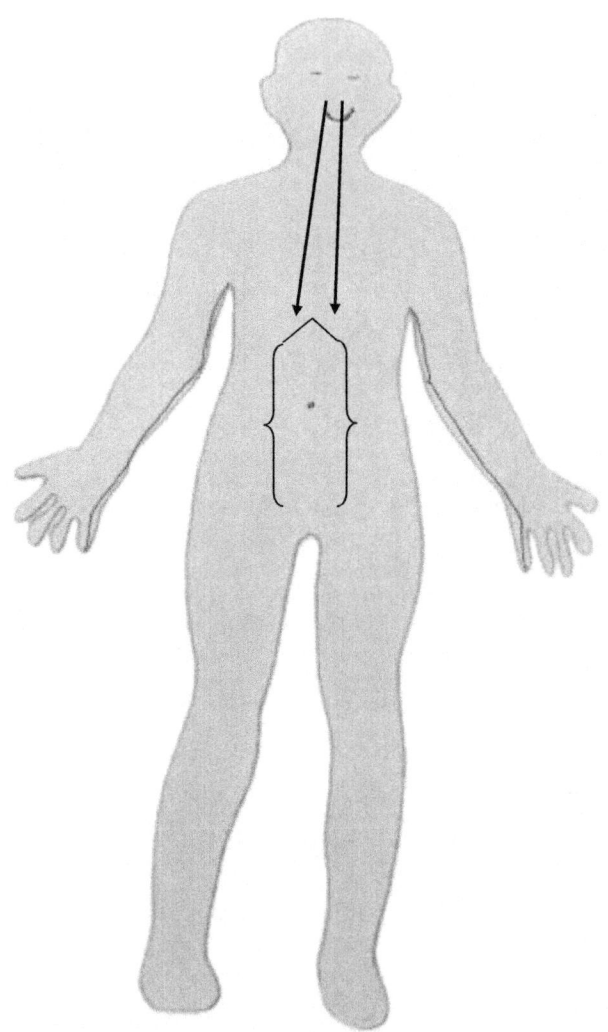

Breathe into the V of your rib cage, and fill your belly with breath

Feeling Joy and Satisfaction
The Solar Plexus Chakra
Your confidence, ambition, and power

It Is About How You Express Your 'Wants'

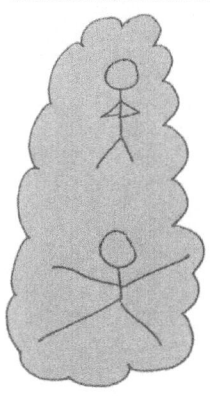

Is your energy too rigid and closed?

OR

Is your energy too big and open?

**Your
Shen Shine**

The Mental Body Energy Field can be seen as the sun's rays shining or raindrops falling on your head

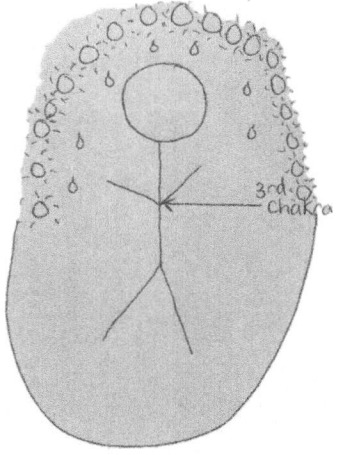

Lower leg discomfort. (Your second heart)

Undervaluing yourself regularly or lack of depth with others

Stiffness in the shoulders. Swollen throat

Scents of bergamot, lime, or grapefruit

Yellow colours or food (turmeric and ginger)

Open your solar plexus area by lifting your rib cage

Reflection

Source Light Into Colour
A Partnership of Vibration and Reflection
Opens Up Like A Lotus Flower

The Heart Chakra and the Thymus Gland
Thoracic Region Energy Zone
Lungs and Large Intestine Energy Channels
The Astral Body Energy Field

The power of self-reflection is to settle the mind.
If you know yourself, and what you value,
the happiness follows.

Source Light Into Colour

In China when a person observes a full ring of multicolour amidst wispy white clouds it is known as Foguang – 'Buddha's Halo'. In India this unworldly sighting is known as Akash Atura - 'Sky Aura'. Until I experienced a transformational climb up Mount Emei, near Chengdu China in 2016, I had not ever considered a circular rainbow to be anything other than a rainbow. I now know it has a name in English also – 'Saints Halo'. These phenomenon are said to be a delightful dance of sunlight with water painting the sky vibrant colours. The colours are believed to be a symbol of how evolved towards self-awareness the observer is.

At the start of my two-year sabbatical in Sichuan, Western China I had spontaneously taken a trip at 5am to Mount Emei. I took a 90 minute bus ride from Chengdu to the base of the mountain. As I stepped off the crowded, noisy, hard-seated bus I read a public notice sign "Remember, climbing Mount Emei isn't just about reaching the summit – it's about the journey, the monasteries, and the breathtaking views along the way. Enjoy your adventure." Well, I immediately started crying!

At approximately 7,000 feet into my ascent, I noticed I was alone. I have no idea for how long I had been walking solo, but I do know I was enjoying a feeling of contentment. 'In the moment' I repeated to myself on every exhale while lifting my face toward the summit. A cheeky macaques monkey scuttled over to my feet, looked at me, jumped up onto a ledge and presented to me the most amazing sight I have ever encountered. A valley that opened up between two steep edges, overlooking white clouds. I honestly thought I was at the end of the earth. I couldn't see anything above, I couldn't see anything below. I could see the dawn of the sun showing many rays, opalescent against the dark earth at the edge of the farthest peak. I didn't want to blink in case I was imagining the sight – a colourful circle of light atop the sea of clouds where in the centre I saw a shadow of what I can only describe as the shape of a human. I felt sick. It was incredible.

The cheeky monkey stayed with me for a short while. I laughed a little, thinking 'Just me, myself, and Emei'. Once I realised the chill in the atmosphere, I decided to continue the walk up the pathway towards the monastery ahead. On arrival I awkwardly spoke to a lovely man of what I had just witnessed.

"Do not feel uncomfortable. You should feel proud."

After our conversation I quickly wrote down in my travel journal the words he had said to me:

"Just as the radiant essence of light can pierce the darkness of the physical environment, the buddha's light can dispel the darkness of our ignorant mind so that we can clearly see the meaning of life, its aim, and direction. What you have seen can draw attention, guide you home, relieve you from fear, and give you wisdom, hope, peace, and joy."

'The radiant essence of light' carries profound symbolism in the East and embodies many meanings:

- **Guidance:** The path of light is said to help lost souls find their way in life.
- **Hope:** The idea of an inner light illuminating the path toward enlightenment. 'Light at the end of the tunnel.'

- **Inspiration:** Light brings clarity to thoughts, sparking creativity. 'A lightbulb moment'.
- **The very essence of existence:** Life depends on the radiant power of light.

But what is light? Glow worms produce light, a fire emits light, and of course the sun radiates light. These are examples of source light. Interestingly, although the moon radiates powerful energy, it is not actually a source of light - it acts as a mirror to reflect light from the sun. Source light travels in straight lines extremely fast. In fact source light is the fastest movement in the universe at approximately 186,282 miles per hour! All light, including generated electrical light from a lamp for example, is electromagnetic wavelength radiation that stimulates sight and makes things bright. It passes through the lens of the eye to the retina at the back of the eye where it is changed to electrical signals that travel through the optic nerve to the brain. Naturally and organically this amazing process happens constantly, without you even thinking about it, every millisecond of everyday.

Do you know your body permanently reflects coloured light? When sunlight enters a droplet of water the wavelengths bend and split into different visible colours that are reflected back out as multicolour. Your fully grown body is approximately 65 - 70% water. The amount of water can change slightly, but the average composition is:
- 73% of your heart is water,
- 83% of your lungs is water,
- your kidneys are 79% water,
- and even your bones have a constitution of 31% water,
- your skin is composed of 64% tiny water droplets.

Water droplets in and on your body play a magical role in creating a rainbow. When high vibrational frequency wavelengths from source enters the water of your body it refracts (bends) and slows down as it passes from air to denser and much lower vibrational frequency energies. Inside each water droplet the light separates into the seven colours of the spectrum, becoming a wiggly wavelength. Depending on the vibrational frequency of the water droplet, the electromagnetic radiation wavelengths are absorbed and then bounce off the inner wall of the water droplet, reflect back out in an arc shape forming a beautiful almond spectrum of colour surrounding your body. This type of rainbow is also known as an aura, or energy field. The brightness of these coloured curves are also generated by the vibrational energy frequencies within your body.

So why do we not see the rainbow around people? Well actually we do have the ability, but most of us have forgotten how. We very often sense the aura, but only when we pay attention.

A Partnership of Vibration and Reflection
Opens Up Like A Lotus Flower

When your chakras are balanced and you feel healthy your entire aura can stretch out to a few metres in radius, glowing very bright in colour. But your energy field can be very small and dull when your chakras are out of balance.

Each colour around us has its own wavelength and unique frequency that can connect to other energies, especially emotional energy. Warm colours typically stimulate the emotions and cool colours give a calming effect on moods. If you're noticing a specific colour brings a good feeling, ie your favourite colour, it is believed to represent your emotional state, or your soul shade, in that particular moment.

Red colours are energetic and fiery. Typically if you are attracted to the colour red you are said to be outspoken and quick at putting thoughts into actions.

Orange colours are attractive to creative, action oriented and positive outlooks. You tend to learn lessons from experience rather than theory and you are said to be independent and realistic.

Yellow colours are associated to a sunny, charismatic and confident personality and symbolise a magnetic energy that attracts a lot of optimism.

Green is the colour of love, compassion, and forgiveness. Attraction to the colour green symbolises a love of nature, music, and not being tied down. You can, however, be easily influenced by environmental situations or by other people.

Pink colours are kind, caring and loving. If you are attracted to pink you live from the heart.

Blue is powerful, insightful, and flowing. You can be said to be 'in the clouds', but you can also be very instinctive and able to communicate what you need to say clearly.

Purple represents being intuitive and empathetic. Attraction to this colour shows you have some psychic and intuitive abilities, with great mental depth.

Indigo portrays a sensitive and empathic soul. You easily absorb thoughts, feelings, emotions, and traumas of others, leading to overwhelm in your own energies.

White shows you are wise, pure, and spiritually connected. Although you have a tendency for perfection, you have a strong sense of connection to something bigger than yourself and everything around you.

Black is typically associated to feeling tired and low. A sign that part of your personality is exhausted, and you are holding on to negative thoughts.

Multicolours show you are busy, energised, and confident. Attraction to multicolours is a sign that you are going through a super busy time, or in the midst of change.

Energy fields are very much recognised in science today. Different research methods, such as Electro Photography, prove the electromagnetic field exists, and clearly show the changes of colour in the aura in response to emotional, physical, and environmental changes. Eastern philosophy recognises the aura as a reflection of your inner state and it plays a vital role in how you communicate with your outer world – you attract other living energies and situations with the relative energy of your energetic field. Simply put, what you project out always comes back to you. Therefore, it is important to take time and self-discipline to manage your inner vibrations effectively, so then your inner world can open up to the world around you, attracting only the energy that you want to receive.

Have you noticed in most Eastern traditions the lotus flower is present. In Hinduism, Buddhism, Islam, and Confucianism to name a few, the lotus flower holds a deep symbolic meaning of purity, resilience, and the journey towards enlightenment. Across many cultures and religions the lotus flower represents spiritual awakening. The flower emerges from muddy waters, slowly opening up to the world. As the lotus blooms each petal absorbs light and in turn they become colourful and beautiful.

We can take a lesson from the lotus flower. If we balance our vibrations and let the reflections of our light shine, we unconsciously allow others to do the same. Our own self awakening creates ripples onto others, and those ripples can be huge.

The Heart Chakra and the Thymus Gland

The heart chakra, also known as Anahatha and the 4th chakra, is related to social identity, unconditional love, and self-protection. It allows us to connect deeply, feel compassion, and develop a sense of peace and contentment.

Every living thing needs love to survive – love is the universal force that runs through us all. An open heart chakra allows a person to love and, more importantly be loved. The heart chakra's purpose is to become open to love and compassion, both to yourself and those around you, and as such it is rightfully known as the 'Seat of the Soul'. Looking after others, giving tender loving care, and ensuring others' needs are met can nourish the soul, and although you might think this is selfless and therefore a strong act of kindness, it is important to be careful because putting others first too often, to your own detriment, can put an energy block at the heart chakra which usually ends up making you feel lonely, insecure and isolated.

Positive thoughts and positive emotions activate the heart chakra, and as a result you naturally feel strong, healthy, and happy. But if the vibrational frequency of 639Hz is off kilter the heart chakra can become easily damaged or wounded which impacts the core of your true self. Negative thoughts have a huge impact on the body's energy, and as such the heart chakra relies heavily on the thymus gland to balance unhappiness.

The thymus gland, located between the two lungs just in front of and above your heart, is majorly important during foetal growth and into childhood for the production of T cells, a type of white blood cell that develops and protects your immune system. It is strongly active up to the age of around 14 years, after then the thymus gland is active as an emotional balancing tool – it grows when happy, and shrinks in times of conflict.

Also known as the 'Gland of Happiness' because it is believed to be powerful in protecting the emotions when the mind, body and soul are in moments of change and adaptation, the thymus gland biologically responds and protects us from negative energy. It secretes the hormone thymopoietin which fuels the production of T-cells in children and in adults it tells the pituitary gland to release antidiuretic hormones. Antidiuretic hormones are the link to your emotions and fluid loss. They regulate water balance in the body (such as sweating, blowing your nose, and the concentration of urine) which is why we tend to get sick when we are deeply unhappy.

You know when your heart chakra is activated and your thymus gland is 'happy' because you feel good. You notice:

√ You are open to all safe and healthy experiences in life

√ Life challenges seem easy to resolve

√ You feel connected to yourself, to your surroundings, and to the natural world.

A blockage of energy at the heart chakra can lead to physical issues such as:

- high or low blood pressure
- upper back, chest, shoulder, arm, and wrist pain
- poor circulation
- chest pains
- respiratory issues

Emotional symptoms can become present when a heart chakra blockage is prolonged. You could experience antisocial behaviours such as:

- a fear of intimacy

- subconsciously creating situations to push love away
- becoming withdrawn from society
- giving too much self-worth and little or zero worth to other people.

Before physical or emotional issues show, a blocked heart chakra can present as phycological issues such as:

- co-dependency with poor boundaries
- jealousy of someone else receiving love and attention
- needing of constant reassurance and love

Happiness nurtures the heart chakra. Other ways to balance energy at the heart chakra include envisioning the colour green glowing in the middle of your chest allowing you to first love yourself, then expanding outward to others. Eating green foods like kale, spinach, green beans, kiwi, green grapes, edamme beans, limes, and avocados are said to be good for the soul. Scents of rose and orange helps you feel connected. Placing green jade, green calcite, watermelon tourmaline, or emerald quartz crystals in the palm of your hand can release positive energy to the heart chakra.

The most impactful way to balance energy at the heart chakra and thymus gland is to balance the love and appreciation that you give to others with the love and appreciation that you give to yourself. Journaling helps in discovering what isn't always obvious – just a simple 5 minute 'end of the day' note to write down what or who you are thankful for and why. Overtime this practise can help you to notice a pattern of self-identity, appreciation, and a feeling of love and compassion.

In modern society it is too easy to be self-critical and attach unworthiness to your self-identity – that deep rooted secret feeling of 'If I play a little small other people will more likely approve of me'. This is the people pleasing aspect of your identity and is a massive factor in the negative internal chatter of "I want to be loved". Quite often, in the West, we are afraid to show who we truly are. Eastern philosophy cautions that if you are playing small then you are attracting the people who negatively play you down when you do show the bigger you. Don't hold yourself back. With a little bit of loving kindness and compassion for yourself, and those you are connected to, you will make your soul light shine with happiness, peace, and contentment.

Thoracic Region Energy Zone

Your back is the pillar of your being. It gives support and strength, uprightness and dignity. Your chest is where reaction and survival patterns build up, where the deep 'I' questions arise: Who am I? What is my I? What is my purpose?

Ancient Eastern philosophers name the chest and upper back area as the 'adaptation tool'. As your emotional body changes through life experiences, the thoracic region energy needs to adapt and change with you. It needs to adapt, otherwise it gets stuck. For example, can you remember a time when your life changed, such as a change in job or promotion, a new relationship, a new home, or a change in lifestyle, and you've continued speaking and thinking as you did in your previous situation, expecting and reacting with the same intentions. At some point did you realise you felt your chest tight, your shoulders rolling forward, and your eyes become heavy with dull headaches. Did you put these physical sensations down to stress – the stresses of something new?

Discomfort in the chest and upper back area can be linked to a manifestation of not being open to adapting to change, of creating old patterns and unconsciously dumping issues or feelings that you don't want to deal with in that moment. Eastern traditions regard this as 'losing touch with decision making'. This area is associated to self-protection, and is manifested in a resistance to asking for support, a resistance to being vulnerable, and a strong sense of pride. These are known as an 'illusion of the self', or you may recognise it as "I'm scared but I am not admitting it." Interestingly, where do you point to when you refer to yourself? It doesn't matter what culture, what language, and what age, most people instinctively point to the sternum, naturally placing the palm of a hand onto the chest area.

A really lovely energy opener in the thoracic region is to gently tap the 'I' zone. With your fingers of one hand held together, tap one strong and two soft taps in a continuous rhythm on the sternum, just above the breast bone. Repeat this 3 tap sequence 21 times and begin to notice the internal vibrations relax the inner tension.

Another great energy opener at the thoracic region is to simply draw your shoulders back. I don't mean squeeze your shoulder blades together so your chest sticks out. I mean to slide your shoulder blades so you are stretching and lengthening the rotator cuff muscles.

Take a moment now to open your chest...

- Start by pulling tall through the crown of your head. Imagine your spine is a pearl necklace extending from the crown of your head right down to your tailbone. As you don't want the pearls to touch, you need to pull the string at the crown of your head upward so you are standing taller with a nice double chin – not looking down or up but looking directly ahead so you are opening the base of your skull. At the same time pull the string at your tailbone to lengthen towards the heels of your feet, opening the space in the middle and lower back.
- Keeping that lift, allow your shoulders to relax and pull back by physically sliding your shoulder blades down. Imagine you have a torchlight embedded in the gap at the front of your collarbone – your clavicle. The beam of light should shine forward. If you are sticking your chest out, the light beam will direct upwards, and similarly if you are heavy in your ribs the light beam will be directed downwards.

- Now, as you take a deep breath in to fill your lungs, feel the V at the front of abdomen (where the two sides of ribs meet) lift. It is a sensation of 'opening' the chest from the diaphragm without peacocking or sticking your chest out. The full breath and the V opening allows your diaphragm to massage your solar plexus chakra. Exhale a long breath to completely empty the lungs to the very last drop of air. Don't allow your spine to collapse, rather continue pulling tall through your spine while sliding your shoulders back and down to open the energy at the collarbones.

Opening the chest not only helps to release acute internal stress, but it also allows your lungs to take in more air, enhancing circulation and boosting your immune system. And along with beautiful posture in your chest and upper back area, a chest stretch also gives your skin a glowing 'Shen Shine'.

Lungs and Large Intestine Energy Channels

Throughout this book so far we have looked at how the internal body energy channels are the subtle pathways of prana energy absorbed from the universe (predominantly the sun), Qi energy from movement and breathing, and Jing energy from digestion of absorbed foods and water; which all operate very closely with the body's chakras and their associated organs, influencing their corresponding hormones. At the source of these subtle pathways of internal body energy there are three main energy channels: Sushumna, Pingala, and Ida. These three main channels carry vital life force prana energy and are directly related to the sympathetic and parasympathetic nervous systems that deal with your mind, body, and soul qualities. Wellness of the entire mind, body, and soul trinity determines how much prana energy can be successfully transformed internally to project a radiant shine - your Shen Shine.

You can stimulate these three main energy channels through nasal breathwork, which can also have a very real effect on your mind, body, and emotions. But it isn't 'just' breathing through the nose that benefits you. The nostril you choose to breathe though can have a huge impact on your absorbed and projected energies too. Rhythms of left or right nostril breathing, known as 'nasal cycles', influence how you behave, how you operate, and how you present yourself to others.

Sushumna, located in the middle of your spinal cord, is the messenger of prana energy. It connects your root chakra and your crown chakra. Your other five main chakras are located along Sushumna where your Tripple Burner energy channel connect to it and receives its energy from it to feed the other energy channels.

To the left of Sushumna within your spinal cord lies Ida and to the right of Sushumna is Pingala.

Ida reflects lunar energy from the moon. It is the main channel for governing water functions including tissue development and waste elimination control during sleep, and it is responsible for your whole body to be nourished of energy. Ida is said to govern speech. Left nostril breathing is said to nurture your emotions, calm your nerves, and assist in silencing the chatter in your mind. When your left nostril is flowing you should avoid intense activities and opt for more calming practises like reading, gentle movement, and going to the toilet.

Pingala reflects solar energy from the sun. It is the main digestive channel and is said to govern smell. Pingala activates critical thinking skills and stimulates the rational and practical self, promotes stamina and vitality, and revives your body's dynamic energy. When your right nostril is flowing you should avoid lounging and relaxing and opt for more physical activities like eating, aerobic movement, and mental activity that requires clear analysis and evaluation.

It is a mystical knowing across all Eastern healing traditions that energy above the shoulders crosses over, and therefore Pingala inhalation through the right nostril stimulates the left side of the brain – the rational, practical self, and Ida inhalation through the left nostril stimulates the right side of the brain – the creative, reasoning and problem solving self.

Take a moment now to focus on your breathing, make sure to be breathing through your nose rather than through your mouth. Put the back of one hand directly under your nose. Do you notice on your out breath the air from one nostril is flowing more dominant, or perhaps even one nostril is blocked. In half an hour or so check your nasal exhalation again and you might notice the dominant nostril has changed. In contemporary living standards the nasal cycle change is believed to be, on average, every 25 minutes, but actually ancient Eastern philosophers endorsed the change to occur every 8 hours in an aim to balance nasal airflow in relation to the external energy changes.

Ancient scriptures state 'In order to maintain harmony of the opposing lunar and solar energies it is best to practise left nostril breathing during the day to balance the internal lunar energy when the body is being vitalised by the sun, and practise right nostril breathing during the night to balance the internal solar energy when the moon's energy is dominant.'

Both Ida and Pingala are rulers of the yin and yang energy channels. Ida refers to Yin energy. Pingagla refers to Yang energy. The lungs energy channel is yin, and the large intestine energy channel is yang. These two energy channels are connected to the heart chakra and both play a vital role in the cleansing of prana energy.

Your two lungs are the main functioning organs when breathing. When you inhale air, your lungs expand. The air entering through your nose or mouth warms and moistens and then travels down your windpipe, located directly behind your oesophagus in your throat, to your bronchial tubes that separate your windpipe and your two lungs. The moistened warm air then enters your expanded lungs, and continues to travel into your alveoli (air sacs) where oxygen from the air is passed into your bloodstream and carbon dioxide (which is a waste product from Jing energy processes) moves from your blood to your alveoli. Your lungs are now at full expansion capacity, and in response your diaphragm and chest wall muscles begin to contract. The shrinking of your lungs and alveoli forces the carbon dioxide to move into the lungs where it combines with the inhaled warm air and is then pushed up through the bronchial tubes and windpipe to exit the body as an exhalation.

Because of the massive number of alveoli, approximately 300 million in each lung, the ability to fully expand your lungs to full, or nearly full, capacity increases the amount of gas exchange into and out of the lungs. Therefore, the more oxygen you can absorb through the alveoli and the more waste gases you can get rid of, the less toxic waste you have remaining in your bloodstream and the more energised and vibrant you feel and look.

Amazingly, although the left lung is slightly smaller than the right, due to 2/3rds of the heart organ sitting on the left side of the body, the left lung still contains the same amount of alveoli as the right lung. The base of the left lung has a little indentation that hugs the base of the heart. This connection of the left lung and heart is believed to be the bridge between the Seat of the Soul (the heart chakra) and the Gland of Happiness (the Thymus gland) with the glow of wellness (Shen Shine) from the skin. Eastern philosophy regards the skin as the third lung, and believe deeply cleansing the skin regularly is just as important for cleansing the mind and the body as is taking a deep, full breath.

The lungs energy channel originates just above the heart and runs down the centre line to connect with the large intestine. It then loops to run up through the diaphragm where it splits into two, one line to each lung. It runs directly up in a diagonal angle into the centre of each lung to then run diagonally again to connect as one line at the heart chakra, running up to the throat where it branches again to each armpit. The lungs energy channel then runs down the inner upper arm, across the inner elbow crease, down the major artery of the internal side of the wrist to run all the way to the tip of the thumb. Indications of requiring stimulation within your lungs energy channel are: asthma symptoms, coughs or wheezing, nasal congestion, white spots on nails, and shoulder pain, The lungs energy channel is associated to absorbing life or wanting to push life away. It is about living life for yourself rather than letting someone else have power over you.

The large intestine is the Yang organ paired with the Yin lungs, and both are important detox organs. The large intestine is the final part of the digestive system and is made up of three parts: the colon, the rectum, and the anus. The whole of the large intestine surrounds the small intestine in a shape similar to a question mark. Running 6 feet long, and 3 inches wide the colon runs from your right lower abdominal (the cecum where it connects to the small intestine), up the outer right side of your abdominal cavity (the ascending colon), across to the left side running underneath the length of the diaphragm (the transverse colon), and down the outer left side of your abdominal cavity (the descending colon) where it then becomes the rectum as it gently moves inward while passing the back of the left hip toward the centre back of your pelvis (the anus) and finally through the sphincter to release waste. The large intestine is known as the mind, body, and soul cleansing organ due its very important role of absorbing liquid and releasing any food, toxins, and emotions that are no longer needed – the matter is finished with, ready to be eliminated.

The large intestine energy channel originates from the outside corner of your index fingernail and runs up the edge of your index finger to the two tendons of your thumb at your wrist. From there it traces your lower arm to your elbow where it continues up the outside of your arm to the back of your clavicle (collar bone) and up the side of your neck and jaw where it internally curves to run over your top lip all the way to your nostril. An imbalance in the large intestine energy channel can cause constipation, diarrhoea, colitis, acidic body ph, smelly or bloody stools, burning anus, accumulated mucus, bloating, a lack of energy, bottling up emotions, rigid thinking, and a resistance to change - clinging to the old.

Nadi Shodhana, also known as Alternate Nostril Breathing, is brilliant for cleaning the lungs and large intestine energy channels. It is exactly what the name says – breathing in through one nostril and then exhaling through the other. By activating the parasympathetic nervous system it helps you feel calm and relaxed, while activating your sympathetic nervous system it sharpens your focus and energy making you feel refreshed and alert. Here's how to do it:

- Sit comfortable with nice posture (don't slouch) and give your nose a good blow into some tissue – give it a good clean first.
- Use your right thumb to close your right nostril and inhale through your left nostril
- At full lung capacity release your right nostril and close your left nostril with your right ring finger
- Exhale completely to the last drop of air
- Inhale through the right nostril to full lung capacity
- At full lung capacity release your right ring finger and use your right thumb to close your right nostril
- Exhale to the very last drop of air through your left nostril
- Repeat the inhalation through your left nostril, then exhale through your right nostril, then inhale through your right nostril, to finish the round by exhaling through your left nostril.
- Repeat as many times as you feel you need.

It is important to not force the breath. You might find one

nostril is completely blocked or resistant to inhale or exhale, this is normal. Keep practising because your body will quickly adjust. Ancient Eastern teachings regard alternate breathing as a tool to balancing a deviated septum, and a great way to notice flashes of visible colours, or 'energy orbs', in your energy field. When you begin to notice the colours it is believed to be a representation of your inner world releasing to your outer world, projecting your true self in that moment, just like a Saints Halo representing how self-aware you are.

The Astral Body Energy Field

All living forms, including trees, plants, and insects, have their own electromagnetic energy fields surrounding and interacting with the physical form. The seven energetic energy fields are also known as aura layers and are connected to frequencies from source light. All layers are active at all times and can influence your physical, mental, and emotional states. Basically, the aura layers are like bubbles of light surrounding you in an oval shape, each bubble big enough to cover you from head to toe. Each layer is always expanding and contracting in bright or dull colours depending on the wellbeing of its corresponding chakra and its associated energetic functions within your physical body. The odd numbered chakras emanate an organised structure of yang energy in the corresponding aura, while the even numbered chakras emanate a yin energy and are more fluid in nature. This creates balance and harmony.

Much of the energetic interaction with other living forms takes place from the Astral Body Energy Field. This auric layer is known as the 'bridge between the physical and spiritual planes' because it assists you when interpreting perception of situations to a more grounded, realistic aspect of reality, and it lifts your soul to a higher level. Eastern teachings describe the Astral Body Energy Field as the layer of love and relationships – love and relationships with others, yourself, and your physical body.

The quality of your Astral Body Energy Field is reflective of your level of self-awareness. An underdeveloped Astral Body layer will have a cloudy, dusky rose colour, while the more self-aware you become the more clear and rose pink your Astral Body layer becomes.

Your Astral Body Energy Field is connected to your heart chakra. It becomes stronger through loving, intimate relationships, but can be weaker during times of conflict. This auric layer shines approximately 12 inches from the skin, and contains the most powerful healing energies - it is where we store our capacity for universal love. Some ancient teachings say this layer requires vulnerability and trust for the self-protection of the heart chakra to surrender.

People with clear bright rose aura are known for their loving and compassionate nature. This energy field is all about displaying warmth and appropriate affection towards others, and as such they are drawn to being sensitive to the emotions of others, making excellent listeners and empathetic souls.

Developing awareness of your astral body energy field is the basis of advancing towards self-development, and the best way to let your protecting heart allow the development is through an awareness of what makes you smile in the present moment.

- **'Walking Meditation'**: A practise that allows you to clear your mind and helps you to be in the present moment. Instead of sitting in a 'trance state' (to quote my friend who regularly enjoys walking meditation), when walking you can easily pay attention to your body and your surroundings without stressing that you are, or are not, meditating correctly. When walking solo you can simply float into your own mediation at any time and at any location. As you walk, notice how your mind tends to drift from one thing to another. Acknowledge these passing thoughts without any judgement. Gently guide your attention back to the physical sensations: the air filling your lungs, your feet on the ground, and how you are holding your hands. Soften your gaze and look downward about six feet in front of you. Begin walking at half your normal speed with slightly smaller steps. Continue to open your awareness of your body while noticing the sensations of your skin – the temperature, the air surrounding you, and if you are outdoors feel the elements on your face. Initially walking meditation might feel strange, but with regular practise you will adjust and notice some incredible insights.

- **Positive affirmations:** "I live in balance with others."

- **Become comfortable focusing on 'you':** Prioritising your own needs and desires rather than those of other people doesn't mean you are actively working against others. It just means you are making time to focus on what makes you happy. Start by politely declining commitments that don't align with your values or interests. Be kind by offering to do something else instead though. Remember, focusing on yourself isn't selfish – it is essential for your overall wellbeing and the quality of your relationships with others.

Ultimately, the energy associated to the heart chakra and the astral body energy field requires kindness and compassion. Take moments to reflect on the meaning of your life – understand what truly matters to you and remember that your energy can draw attention, guide you home, relieve you from fear, and give you wisdom, hope, peace, and happiness.

"Be like the lotus: trust in the light, grow through the dirt, believe in new beginnings." Hua Mulan

Side of Your Body: The Large Intestine Energy Channel
(the channel runs on both sides of your body)

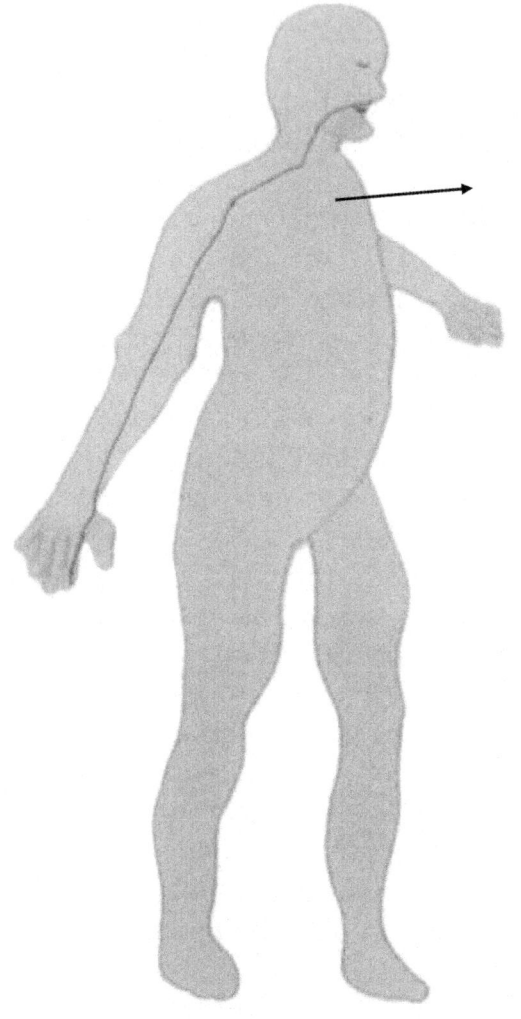

Slide your shoulder blades down your back to open your chest

Front of Your Body: The Lungs Energy Channel.

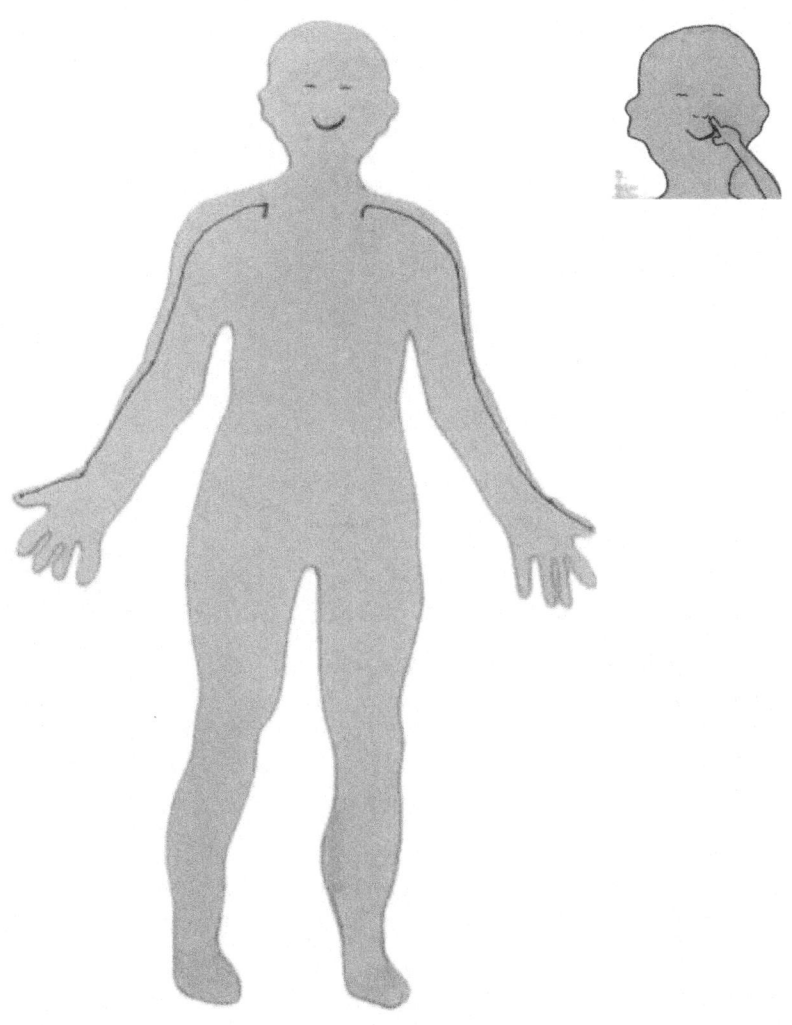

Clean the lungs and large intestine energy channels with alternate nostril breathing. Nadi Shodhana also helps you feel calm and relaxed while refreshed and focused.

Feeling Happiness and Kindness
<u>The Heart Chakra</u>
Your social identity, vulnerability, and self-awareness

<u>It Is About How You Give and Receive Love</u>

Do you give too much?
OR
Is your love all for yourself?

Water

The Astral Body Energy Field can be seen as bouquets of roses or a broken bridge between love and relationships

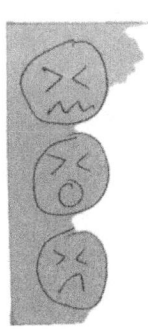

Chest or upper back discomfort

A resistance to change
Co-dependancy with a need for constant reassurance

Respiratory problems or poor circulation

Scents of rose or orange

Green colours or food (kale, spinach, or kiwi)

Journaling helps to discover patterns

Balance

Psyche
Sound Is The Universe In Beautiful Song

The Thyroid Glands and the Throat Chakra
Throat Centre Energy Zone
Liver and Gallbladder Energy Channels
Etheric Template Energy Field

Music not only changes your mood,
it changes the way you think and
how you present yourself to the world.

Psyche

The term 'psyche' dates back to ancient times when it was, and still is, used as a description of personal thoughts, feelings, motivations, and reactions to social and physical influences. In older texts, the word 'soul' is used to represent the psyche, and is said to maintain a balance between opposing qualities of conscious and unconscious thoughts, feelings, motivations, and reactions of the self and others.

Ancient Eastern philosophy believes every new born is given the 'psyche' as an inherent blueprint for life, both physically and mentally, equipping the body and the mind with patterns of behaviour. It is said to be the 'Self' - a person's character separate from the ego or personality, but deeply rooted in biology of evolution inherited through the nervous system.

The nervous system is the body's major communicating system that controls and regulates other systems within your body. It functions as two main parts - the Central Nervous System and the Peripheral Nervous System. Both are the foundation of all activity including movement, thought, reactions, and memory. The central nervous system keeps your psyche in communication with your inner and outer environments with electrical signals called nerve impulses that are transmitted to the brain via the spinal cord. Outside of the central nervous system there are millions of sensory receptors that detect changes occurring both inside and outside your body, this is your Peripheral Nervous System (PNS). Through its sense receptors your peripheral nervous system maintains balance within your body's organs, including your brain, and various tissues including bone, fascia, and muscle. It monitors light and sound, scent, taste and touch and the variations of pressures and vibrations throughout your body.

Information gathered from sense receptors in the peripheral nervous system runs through the Vagus Nerve. This massive nerve is important for digestion, breathing, immune response, temperature regulation, and the control of mucus and saliva production. It is a long winding pathway throughout the trunk of your body from the lower part of your brain, through the neck where it branches into the left vagus nerve and the right vagus nerve. The left vagus nerve enters the thorax between your carotid artery and jugular vein and descends to the diaphragm. The right vagus nerve enters the right lung and descends to the chest organs, exiting at the diaphragm to join the left vagus nerve as a single system again, where it enters the stomach and large intestine. As such the vagus nerve is known as 'The Wandering Nerve'.

The vegus nerve is responsible for the functioning of the voice box, the meninges in the outer ear, heart rate, gastrointestinal peristalsis, sweating, and regulating inflammation within the body. It is also understood to be the nerve that stimulates emotional changes, especially the instinctive awareness to others' reactions of your views and ultimately your self-censorship – the emotions connected to the throat chakra.

Sound Is The Universe In Beautiful Song

The throat chakra is said to be the link to verbal communication through sound. Sound allows us to experience the world through vibration.

For as long as civilisation has existed, and before humans had words; sounds, instruments, chanting, and vibrational frequencies have been used as a way to transmit communication – the vibration of sound representing language. Vibrational frequencies in ceremonies and healing sessions have been used in Eastern traditions for aeons to stimulate positive emotional changes within people:

- 936hz opens you up for spiritual and physical connection.

- 852hz allows you to focus on your main goals in life.

- 741 hz makes you feel at one with your 'self' again. It boosts social awareness and emotional intelligence.

- 639hz builds relationships and interaction between loved ones. This is an important frequency to tune in to when you feel misunderstood and to help build tolerance within relationships.

- 528hz is the transformation frequency. It is believed to reduce anxiety and stress and creates a more harmonious state of being by removing impurities that cause sickness and disease. This frequency is found in grass, oxygen, and the buzz of bees. Interestingly, it was the frequency used to clean oil from the Gulf of Mexico during the BP oil spill in 2010.

- 432hz is said to be the natural frequency of the universe. It is also thought to be the frequency found at ancient sites such as the Great Pyramids and Stone Henge.

- 417hz helps welcome positive thoughts and balance. It reduces anxiety and lowers blood pressure and heart rate. It is believed to encourage synchronicity between both hemispheres of the brain, increasing creativity and the ability to fully enjoy life's pleasures.

- 396hz offers the feeling of being at one with your mind, body, and soul. This frequency will guide you if you are feeling disconnected from the world.

Yoga Nidra, a practise of laying on your back and listening to sound while following guidance to open the subconscious and release any energy blockages, is a brilliant way to experience sound vibrational frequencies. The vibrations of Himalayan singing bowls are said to resonate with each of the seven main chakras. There is evidence that yoga nidra helps to relieve mind and body stress, and in recent years it has been positively applied to assist combat soldiers in recovering from post-traumatic stress. At the beginning of the session you set an intention, and during the session the leader guides you to go deep into the reason of that intention.

It was during a Yoga Nidra session in Dharamsala, India, that I met Daniyal, a restaurant manager from central London on a 6-week break to 'prevent a nervous breakdown', as he put it.

Daniyal: "Phhuuhhhhhh. Have you been crying too? "

Me: "I've never cried so much."

Daniyal: "I've done a lot of work on releasing the tension I didn't realise I've been carrying in my body for, probably, years. I find it incredible that it has taken me to come to a third world country where people live a simple life, talk openly about their outlook on reality, hold strangers hands, smile even though they're wearing shoes with holes in the soles, and dance with pleasure when they find something funny... why does it take witnessing and being part of such human instinctive behaviour to realise how self-conscious and, quite frankly, self-obsessed we in the developed world are. It's laughable really."

It was a full moon that night, and I joined Daniyal at a Kirtan celebration. Kirtan is a community practice that involves chanting ancient Sanskrit songs. The correct pronunciation of the Sanskrit language is believed to create vibrations that connect with the subconscious mind and the vibrational sounds of the universe; allowing emotions to flow and release trapped energy.

Well, the whole place partied like it was a millennium... singing, chanting, and playing drums until late. The room was full and the energy was alive. We all hugged, we all held hands, a lot of people cried. Daniyal actually sobbed on my shoulder.

Daniyal: "Medicine for the soul."

The next morning Daniyal, myself and a few others from the Kirtan went to Tsuglhakhang, the main Tibetan temple in Dharamsala to attend a talk by His Holiness the Dalai Lama. We sat directly in front of him... we were close enough to see his cute glasses and sparkly eyes! His laugh was infectious. Such a gorgeous man. As he walked in, the whole temple filled with energy from the chanting of the monks... oh my, I looked at Daniyal as he looked at me - both of us with bright red noses and tears streaming down our faces. I couldn't stop crying, from deep in the back of my throat... one memory I wish to never loose. Unbelievable.

Later, over a hot chai chat, Daniyal explained to me the reason that led him to visit Dharamsala, and how his involvement in the welcoming community there had made him fully aware that his anxiety and bottling up of feelings was actually due to a blockage in his throat chakra. In London he was experiencing difficulty holding conversations and communicating with almost everyone. Any conversation he was able to hold was based on gossiping, dominating conversation, and speaking without thinking – he was often told he did not have a filter. He was aware he had become a 'know it all', but he couldn't seem to control it His tinnitus and mouth ulcers had become painful, which gave him more reason to withdraw from social situations, and although he was aware that his social anxiety was an overreaction, he noticed he had developed a silly cough every time he wanted to speak, which didn't help him. Daniyal instinctively knew that if he didn't take a break, sooner rather than later he would start to breakdown.

I couldn't connect the person sat in front of me as the man Daniyal was describing. As I listened to his story all I could think was "A thousand people could be sat here in silence and stillness, listening as you speak your beautiful song..."

The Thyroid Glands and the Throat Chakra

The throat chakra, located at the base of your throat in the centre of your two collarbones, governs communication, self-expression and truth. It is closely linked to the thyroid gland that secretes Thyroid-Stimulating Hormones (TSH) such as Thyroxine (T4) and Triiodothyronine (T3) which both influence various metabolic functions including energy levels, body temperature, and body weight. If there is too little T3 or T4 hormone detected in your bloodstream, you can begin to show signs and symptoms like:

- Persistent tiredness and lack of energy
- Unexplained weight gain with no significant change in diet or physical activity
- Feeling excessively cold
- Dry skin and brittle hair
- Muscle cramps
- Unusual fluctuations in mood (what you could describe as depression)
- Changes in voice quality

This is known as hypothyroidism. Any diagnosis or ailment with a 'hypo' means 'low levels'. Conversely, any 'hyper' means 'high levels'. Hyperthyroidism is a condition where the thyroid hormones are in excess. Signs and symptoms include:

- Racing or pounding heartbeat
- Unexplained restlessness or anxiety
- A regular need to consciously take deep, controlled breaths (the ones we take when we are feeling nervous)
- Unintentional weight loss, but with a constant appetite
- Upset digestion (sloppy waste)

For your body to make thyroid hormones, your thyroid

endocrine gland needs iodine, which you get from table salt in your food and water. Proper iodine levels in your blood are crucial for metabolism balance, but too little or too much iodine can massively affect your hormone production which consequently impacts on your metabolism. Metabolism is the chemical process in your body that breaks down the food you eat to produce energy that keeps your body functioning optimally. It is a very fine balancing act of chemicals within your bloodstream. When the thyroid gland malfunctions it can affect your whole being, especially the way you express yourself.

The throat chakra is also known as Vissudha, 5th chakra, and The Voice. This chakra's purpose is to regulate communication and honesty by resonating at a frequency of 852hz. It is uniquely individual to each person's needs and truth. Blocked energy here manifests as bottled up feelings that fester within. The throat chakra creates a sense of being part of a community, and when your throat chakra is balanced you notice you are listening to others with a good sense of timing and intonation in your own voice when responding and reacting in conversation. You notice you are confident when speaking, without a sense of restriction or fear of other people's opinions or reactions to your views. You are able to communicate the bigger picture with clarity.

The throat chakra controls the thyroid gland and is connected to the larynx, ears, windpipe, and the upper part of the lungs. A deficiency or blockage in this chakra can lead to physical issues such as

- Neck stiffness
- Teeth grinding
- Laryngitis

- Mouth ulcers
- Ear infections

Emotionally it can be difficult to have conversations when communicating with almost everyone. You can experience

- A fear of speaking, or speak with a weak or small voice
- Gossiping
- Dominating conversation
- Bottling up words or getting tongue tied

Psychologically an unbalanced throat chakra can create issues in your social life. You will start to become self-defensive, which eventually becomes a challenge to having healthy, strong relationships with others because your needs over shadow theirs. There is a thin line between being confident and being overbearing.

The most impactful way to balance energy at the throat chakra is by consciously finding equilibrium between clear speech and knowing when to listen. Although this isn't easy, remember that communication skills are learnable. Be mindful of non-verbal facial expressions, gestures, and tone – how your message is received is just as important of the content of what you are communicating. And, of course, developing your emotional intelligence - understanding the emotions of yourself and others during communication enhances your ability to connect socially.

Other ways to balance energy at the throat chakra include envisioning a peaceful blue colour glowing in the middle of your throat, increasing your ability to communicate. Drink fresh juice and tea, and eat detoxing blue foods like blueberries, blue cheese, Damson plums, blue carrots, and even blue pansies. Interestingly, when eaten fresh, blueberries have the highest antioxidant levels among common vegetables and fruits. Placing turquoise sodalite, celestite, and aquamarine crystals in the palm of your hand can release positive energy to the throat chakra, along with the scents of chamomile or rosemary.

A great 'feel good' way of balancing the throat chakra is, quite simply, through singing songs. By understanding the meaning of the words and how they are presented you can begin to articulate your own way of expressing your own meaning through word choice. Better yet, singing songs out loud and proud engages the vocal muscles, helping to strengthen and enhance breath control, speech quality, and overall emotional expression. Feeling comfortable with your voice contributes to better self-esteem and self-confidence. So get your favourite tunes on when doing mindless activities, especially around the house or when soaking in the bath or shower, and blast your voice out loud and proud. Neale Donald Walsch puts singing into perfect context:

"Singing connects the mind with the heart, and the heart with the soul. So sing, I dare you. Sing!"

The Throat Energy Zone

Your throat is where self-expression resides. Ancient Eastern teachings say the throat is significant to how you express yourself to the world, and its strength, or need to be strengthened, can influence how you articulate your thoughts, feelings, and desires.

Without thinking about it, place your hand on your throat area. 99% of the time when I ask people to do this they instinctively place their index finger and thumb to the lower edges of the jaw line. You may not think about your jaw often, but it is constantly in action. The movement that connects your jawbone, also known as the mandible, and jaw joint, also known as temporomandibular joint (TMJ) requires action from your ears, face, tongue, and the base of your skull. Tension in these areas creates tension in your jaw, which will eventually affect the functioning of your mouth and gastrointestinal tract, and consequently create trapped energy in your throat chakra.

Signs of needing to release tension in your jaw show as:

- Voice definition issues (like having a frog in your throat or needing to cough to clear your voice)
- Throat problems
- An increased heart rate resounding as a strong pounding sensation in the front of your neck, just to the side of your thorax
- Excessively high or low blood pressure seen as a red face or pale complexion
- The gut will tell you it is not happy as well with, what is known as, a 'rotund belly' (belly sticking out)

All of the above signs are quite often passed off as 'tiredness', but actually if throat energy zone problems were looked at closer, the link to emotional and psychological blockages would be clearly seen as:

- Lack of trust
- Lack of nurturing or tender loving care, both platonic and romantic
- An inability to speak true feelings.

If ignored, these emotional and psychological symptoms begin to manifest as physical problems such as:

- Discomfort or pain in the ear, face, jaw, or neck
- Clicking or popping sounds in the ears when opening or closing the jaw
- Difficulty when swallowing smoothly
- Speaking with many 'erm's' or pauses within sentences – making your communication 'boring' for other people
- Reduced facial expressions
- Difficulty to tune into other people's voices – unable to listen

A simple energy opener in the throat chakra will gently relax your jaw. Close your lips while breathing through the nose allowing your jaw to drop, which naturally opens a small gap between your teeth. Rest your tongue on the roof of your mouth behind your upper front teeth and, while relaxing the throat, take conscious deep breaths into the back of your throat. This helps to clear any mucus build up, which frees the swallowing mechanism and allows your throat to open to a full capacity. Repeat this relaxation as often as possible, being aware of the sensations throughout the jaw and surrounding area.

Another great energy opener at the throat energy zone is to open the base of the skull. Here's how to lengthen the vertebrae at the top of your neck to open the space at the back of your head:

- While relaxing the jaw, sit or stand with your shoulders back and chest open.
- Pull your chin straight back and down toward your chest, creating a double chin but keep looking forward.
- Lengthen through the crown of your head to lengthen the spine while gently pressing the shoulder blades flat to open the chest and V of the rib cage.
- Gently turn your head to the left.
- Hold the stretch for 3 seconds, release, and turn your head back to the centre.
- Gently turn your head to the right.
- Hold the stretch for 3 seconds, release, and return your head to the centre.

Have you ever noticed when you are feeling insecure, or self-conscious when communicating with people, that you tend to lift your jaw slightly while compressing the back of your neck and almost jutting your head forward? This is your psyche's way of protecting you from any criticism. By practising this throat energy zone stretch you are gently massaging your negative thoughts away, while also giving your brain a lovely energy boost as well as clearing brain fog. Similarly, by opening up the whole of the spinal column, which opens up the energy channels to your body organs, you are giving an immediate boost to your metabolism, breathing, and waste elimination.

Liver and Gallbladder Energy Channels

The liver plays a crucial role in effective metabolism, breathing, and waste elimination. Among its hundreds of jobs in maintaining good health, the liver gets rid of old red blood cells and clears toxins.

After around 120 days of delivering oxygen and collecting waste products in your bloodstream, aged or damaged red blood cells begin to break down. Your liver filters the aged or damaged red blood cells, from which iron is reused to make new red blood cells; and water, cholesterol, electrolytes (sodium and potassium), and bilirubin combine together to make bile, which is then transported to your gallbladder for storage. Your gallbladder absorbs and send to the kidneys approximately 90% of the water content, and the remaining concentrated acidic bile fluid is stored in the gallbladder until it is required for digestion. Each time you eat food, your gallbladder releases bile back into your liver to be secreted into your small intestine to help break down fats for absorption. As a note here, if your gallbladder has been removed the creation of bile is still the same, it is just a slower process so the liver isn't overwhelmed in having to store the digestive fluid.

Once the fats have been broken down in the small intestine, the bile is then separated. Most of the bile content is reabsorbed into your liver, but bilirubin continues through the digestive process eventually leaving your body in faeces and urine. Interestingly, it is bilirubin that gives your faeces its brown colour and urine its yellow colour. It is also the compound responsible for the yellow colouring of healing bruises, and the yellow colour of your skin when jaundiced.

Urine samples can measure the levels of eliminated bilirubin to give an indication of how well your liver and gallbladder are functioning. High or low levels of bilirubin often indicates a problem with bile clearance and can highlight that either of the two organs are not functioning efficiently, especially in clearing toxins from the bloodstream. Too many toxins in the blood can have significant effects on your psyche, such as confusion, forgetfulness, altered communication patterns, and unexplained irritability or frustration.

Amazingly, it doesn't take long for the immune system to recognise the toxins, and immediately antibodies are produced to protect your tissues and cells from attack. If toxins are in your body for long periods of time – I'm talking weeks – then eventually the antibodies start attacking your thyroid glands, resulting in body processes and functions slowing down. If you notice you are becoming restless and fidgety, nervous, and inappropriately respond to the slightest remark when communicating with other people, then chances are your metabolism is misfunctioning.

Ancient Eastern philosophy recognises altered communication patterns and unexplained irritability or frustration as an energy imbalance at the liver and gallbladder energy channels.

The liver energy channel is a yin energy pathway associated with the nervous system and the thyroid glands, which collectively support your detoxification processes. The liver energy channel originates from the big toe, running up the inner leg, through the groin area, up to the ribcage where it ends. Indications of requiring stimulation within the liver energy channel are: regular eye infections, hepatitis, jaundice, toenail fungal or yellow thickening toenails, hypertension, and skin pimples from slow detoxing processing.

The gallbladder energy channel is a yang energy pathway said to play a role in the health of your muscles and connective tissues. It originates at the outer corner of each eye, runs to the earlobe, continues up towards the temples where it runs over your ears to the back of your head. From there it swoops up along the back of your head to just above each eyebrow, to then descend down the back of the head and neck to the front of your ribcage. It then continues down your waistline to your pelvis and down the outside of your thighs and lower legs to the outer edge of your fourth toe. Indications of excess or deficiency of flowing energy in the gallbladder energy channel can lead to: nervousness, an unrealistic and regular expectation of criticism, and cravings for greasy foods. Physically you can experience TMJ stiffness in the jaw, random discomfort or pain on one side of your head or body, a bitter taste in the mouth, bloating, loose yellow coloured faeces, and excessive flatulence.

A great support for the liver and gallbladder energy channels is a simple, yet massively effective pressure point stimulation named 'The Shoulder Well'. This pressure point sits in the middle of the trapezius, halfway between your shoulder joint and the base of your neck, along the top of each shoulder. To stimulate this pressure point:

- Gently lift the muscle on the very top of your shoulder, between your neck and shoulder ball and socket joint, using your thumb and middle finger of the opposite hand and give it a very gentle shake.
- Using your index finger, press into the middle point on top of the muscle and circle on the spot for 5 seconds.

This quick stimulation can immediately release repressed tension and frustration, and it allows you to focus on softening and easing any mental irritability. Eastern philosophers regard this point as the 'release of pregnancy' – it can induce labour, so for the pregnant ladies please do not lift and press this point just gently stroke the palm of your hand from your jaw line to the end of your shoulder joint while focusing on relaxing the muscle and connective tissues.

Eastern philosophy also regards the liver and gallbladder energy channels as the place where cleansing occurs, and with the development of self-awareness and connecting to your inner self, you can create patterns toward releasing any toxic energy, both physically and energetically.

Etheric Template Energy Field

Everything has a pattern behind it – the way you use your mind, the way your emotions engage, the relationships that you create, all your activities have particular patterns. If you can become aware of your patterns, then you can begin to make changes to form your most successful physical and energetic body; and ultimately the most successful patterns for your thoughts, movements, and feelings.

The etheric template energy field forms a structure of patterns that connect the mind with the nervous system, manifesting in you being well or not so well. The patterns you associate with, such as carelessness or carefulness, narrow-mindedness or broad-mindedness, can have a huge impact on your physical and energetic form. And by 'form' I mean vibrations. You know the old saying 'Thoughts create habits, and habits create beliefs'? Well, for the Etheric Template Energy Field to work in balance with your body and mind, you need to be aware of any patterns that are making your soul feel uncomfortable. This process takes courage, and should be sensitively and kindly performed.

The energy of the fifth auric layer extends up to 2 feet away from the physical body in an oval shape, creating free space for your physical body to move in, and for your energetic body to move through. Eastern philosophy call it the 'Mirror Layer', where energetic vibrations are mirrored onto the physical body, such as body language communicating subtle expressions. In other words, aspects of your identity, personality, and energy flow are shown in the way you move. When you are connected to your soul and you feel you can express your true self, the etheric template energy field will be in its utmost expression, radiating cobalt blue orbs.

In addition to the expression of energetic communication, the etheric template energy field guides development of the physical body. It is believed to exist from conception where it surrounds cells, ensuring proper formation of the physical body. It is also believed that after birth, and throughout life, any ailment or sickness shows up in the physical body long after it has already established in the etheric template. Through acknowledgment of the etheric template energy field, and implementing ways to heal the fifth auric layer, ancient Eastern cultures believe you can avoid much physical, psychological, and emotional discomfort arising.

The best way to bring awareness to your etheric template energy field is by returning to your natural vibration state via natural sound frequencies.

- **'Listen'**: Tuning in to the sounds around you can remind your senses that there is more to this world. Taking a moment to extend your conscious hearing to the wider environment, such as tuning in to the birds singing (which is constant and quite often very beautiful), or the rhythm of continuous movement within your nearby environment (the melodic pattern of the elements or the monotonous hum from vehicles or machinery). Listening to sounds can create a sense of calm and provide reconnection to your own nature.

- **Positive affirmations:** Create your own melodic tune to these words "I communicate with clarity and ease. My voice is necessary."

- **Become aware of your body language:** This involves noticing how you physically interact with others and how they react to your body movements. Practise being intentional with your gestures and facial expressions, paying particular attention to your posture and the signals your arms, fingers, legs, and feet give – it is amazing how positioning your feet in the direction to the person or people you are talking with can unconsciously convey your regard to the worth of the communication, and that value is reflected back to you.

Ultimately though, for the energy at the throat chakra and the etheric template energy field to be balanced and harmonious, and therefore supportive to the liver's optimal functions, you need to be in tune to the softness and sweetness that make your own true nature. Take moments to remind yourself of the pleasing sounds that makes your soul smile and allow your body to move with gentleness and good intention. Quite often vibrational healing sounds such as Himalayan singing bowls, tuning forks, or simply partaking in a good old singsong can ease discomfort and will willingly and instinctively releases toxic energy patterns. By using healing sounds you can influence the energetic pattern within the etheric template which consequently helps restore balance and alignment within your physical body.

"Your body doesn't heal the way we were taught. It doesn't heal through chemicals. You heal via frequencies, vibration, information, and pattern connections." - Dr. Jerry Tennant

Front of Your Body: The Liver Energy Channel.

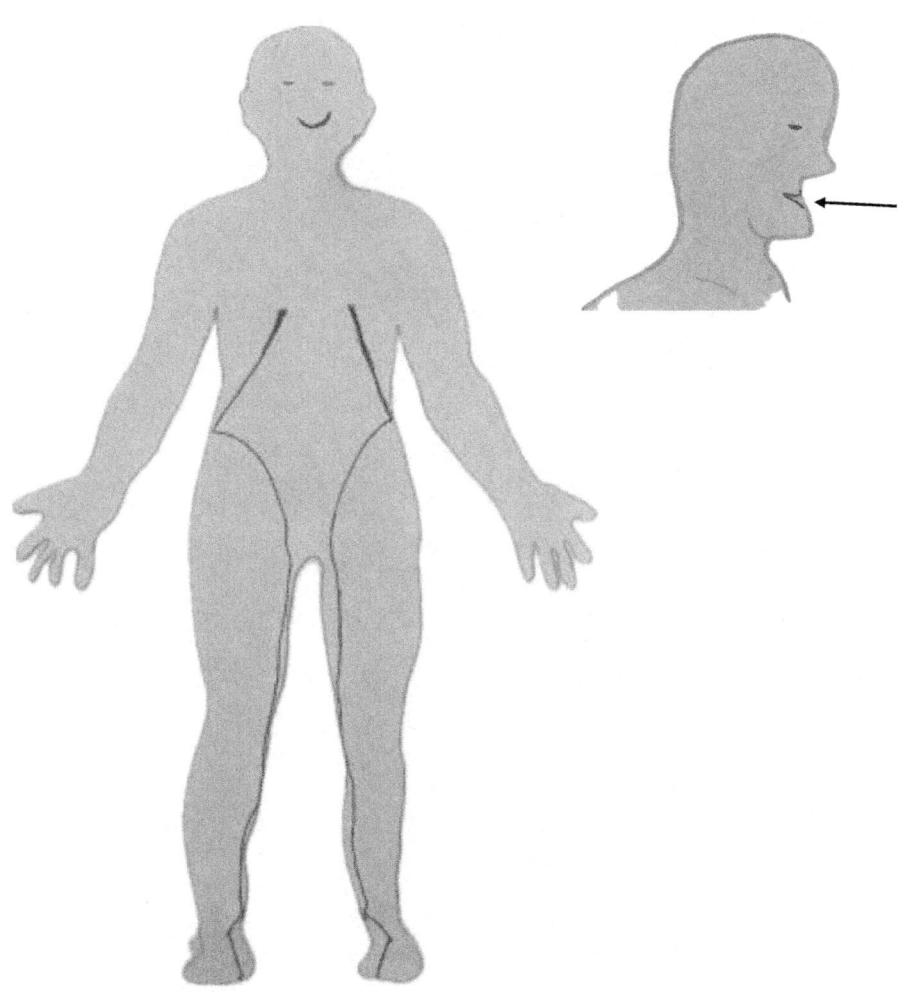

Close your lips and breathe through your nose. Allow your jaw to relax and open a small gap between your teeth. Place your tongue at the roof of your mouth and behind your top teeth. Breathe deeply through your nose to relax your throat

Side of Your Body: The Gallbladder Energy Channel.
(the channel runs on both sides of your body)

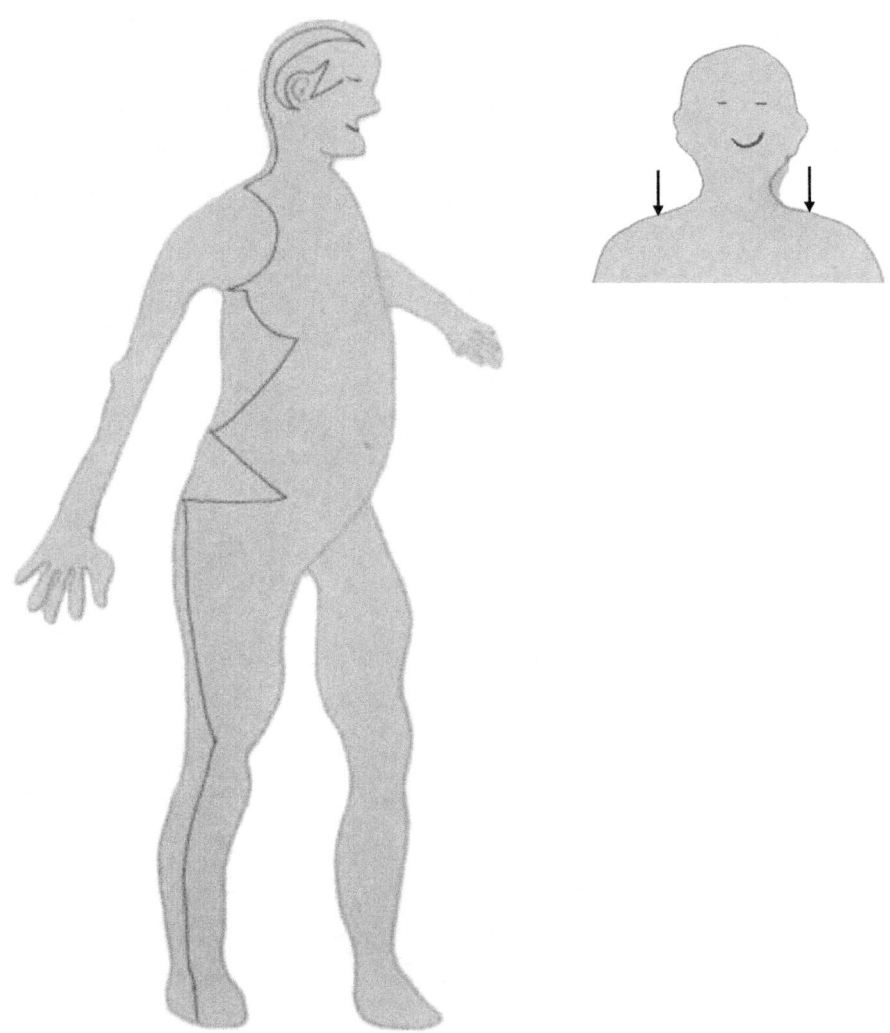

The Shoulder Well Pressure Point (also known as GB21):
Pinch your shoulder muscle with your middle finger and thumb and using your index finger press down directly on top of the muscle to relieve tension and headaches

Ability To Communicate
The Throat Chakra
Your self-expression with benevolent truth.

It Is About How You Express Your 'Needs'

Are you the great pretender?
OR
Do you wear your heart on your sleeve?

Metabolism

The Etheric Template Energy Field can be seen as a mirror reflecting patterns in your thoughts and feelings through your body language

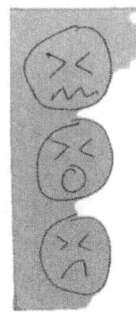

Strong pounding sensations in the front of your throat

Needing to regularly clear your throat when speaking

Face, neck, and ear discomfort

Scents of chamomile or rosemary

Blue colours and foods (blueberries or bluecheese)

Listen to sounds around you to comfort your inner self
Sing loud and proud

Akasha

The Hypothalamus and the Crown Chakra
Ketheric Body Energy Field
Life Energy

Universal Self Care
The Link Between Our Inner World and Our Outer World

You have the right to ask, if you only take the moment.

The Hypothalamus and the Crown Chakra

The brain is an organ made up of nervous tissue within your skull. It is the main communication centre of your nervous system and your endocrine system. Its function is to coordinate the messages received from other organ gland hormones and to organise the correct nerve responses, such as when to move, when to eat, and the appropriate way to interact with other people, according to the state of your mind in that given moment.

The thalamus is a small egg shaped area in the middle of your brain that is essential for the processing of your senses. It filters sensory neurons and motor neurons into 'important information' and 'not important information' – what matters and what doesn't matter. The important motor neuron information is sent to the curly bundle of wrinkles and folds in the superficial part of your brain, known as the cerebral cortex. The cerebral cortex controls memory, thinking, and problem solving – basically the functions of consciousness. The important sensory neuron information is directed to the hypothalamus.

Hypothalamus is a Greek word – thalamus means inner chamber, and hypo means under. Your almond shaped hypothalamus gland sits right underneath your thalamus, just above your pea sized pituitary gland, located behind the bridge of your nose at the base of your brain. In Eastern philosophy it is thought that the pituitary gland and the hypothalamus gland work together in linking the nervous system and the endocrine systems.

There are two main hormones that are solely produced and released by the hypothalamus, without assistance from the pituitary gland. These two hormones are:

- Dopamine - known as the 'reward hormone' because it acts as a feel good messenger helping to stimulate cognitive functions in the brain, and reinforces pleasurable experiences, like when you eat naughty food - that "Ahhhh yessss" sensation you feel when eating chocolate (or is that just me!)
  Dopamine's main role is to help regulate the release of other hormones, such as adrenaline and thyroid stimulating hormones, from the pituitary gland.

- Somatostatin - works to turn off the flow of hormones released from the pituitary gland when they are not needed.

Basically, somatostatin and dopamine are critical hormones for the brain's communication with the pituitary gland to send 'important information' messages for other hormone activation. If your hypothalamus did not create and release dopamine and somatostatin your endocrine system and nervous system would be in chaos.

I often say the body will naturally find the simple way to get what it needs. Four simple ways to naturally get dopamine and somatostatin hormones to release from the hypothalamus are:

1. get regular sufficient sleep,
2. eat healthily,
3. move your body, and
4. increase your positive social interactions with love and compassion.

Simple.

The crown chakra, also known as Sahasrara, 7th Chakra, and The

Thousand Petal Lotus plays a vital role in fostering positive social interactions. When this chakra is balanced it enhances your ability to understand how love, compassion, empathy, and forgiveness brings knowledge, wisdom, and bliss.

Too much energy at the crown chakra can create a lot of issues in your mind. Confusion and overthinking creates difficulty when trying to focus the mind, often resulting in trying too hard to settle thoughts and ultimately ending up in getting nowhere. And if the crown chakra is closed, the thought of universal energy becomes frightening or unlikely to be true. It can be challenging to look at the body as vibrating energy, quite often presenting sceptical or stubborn thoughts.

When you make time each day to focus on settling the complexities of your mind, and you allow thoughts to come and go without too much consideration to the content of those thoughts, you are eventually able to take in and understand fully that there is a deeper meaning to life. Considered the 'Chakra of Enlightenment'; ancient Eastern philosophy regards this chakra as the universal energy from where your purpose in life becomes crystal clear. The crown chakra controls the whole physical being. You know when the energy at your crown chakra is unbalanced because your physical body will generally feel weak in energy.

Unlike the lower six chakras, the crown chakra is not directly associated with a specific endocrine gland, nor is it associated to an organ or energy channel. However, it does massively influence the overall balance and harmony of the hypothalamus and pituitary gland, which affects the whole chakra system, endocrine energy system, the efficient functioning of all internal organs, and the flow of energy channels. Balanced energy at the crown chakra therefore promotes a state of good well-being.

Ancient teachings say the crown chakra isn't actually fully balanced until mid-life. In our modern living standards this age is averaged between 45-50 years old. Having said that, not everyone will fully balance their crown chakra because all the lower six chakras need to be open and balanced before the crown chakra can resonate at its natural frequency of 936Hz.

The most impactful way of helping to balance energy at the crown chakra is to literally do nothing. The crown chakra is associated to silence. Through developing comfort in quietness you can experience moments of prolonged bliss – feelings of pure awareness of being in the present moment. The crown chakra becomes balanced through quietening the constant inner chatter in your head. Laying on your back with your legs straight and hip distance apart, and your arms resting at your sides with palms face up has been practised for centuries to achieve full relaxation and stillness of the mind. It is associated to the brahmarandhra at the crown of the head, where the crown chakra is situated. Ancient Eastern cultures believed that from the brahmarandhra the soul leaves the physical body at the moment of death, and as a consequence this relaxation position symbolises the change from life to death. Also known as 'Corpse Pose', this restful position is a reminder of the necessity to 'listen' – to become aware of the sensations, feelings, and needs of your body in the present moment.

Other ways to assist in balancing energy at the crown chakra include envisioning the colour violet glowing on the top of the head connecting you to a greater energy. Eating good combination foods that balance the acid and alkaline in the digestive processes, and especially eating fresh foods that are properly cooked. Placing amethyst or clear quartz crystals and diamonds in the palm of your hand can release positive energy to the crown chakra, along with the scent of patchouli, labdanum, or frankincense.

Of course not everybody has access to diamonds and clear quartz, so another great 'feel good' way of connecting to the crown chakra is through soaking your feet in a salt bath. This relaxing pamper on your feet has been used for aeons, giving your mind, body, and soul a moment to unwind and relax. Make sure to buy magnesium sulphate (bath salts) rather than the good olde table salt. Dissolve half a cup of bath salts into a large bowl of warm water and soak your feet for 10 to 20 minutes, once a week. Not only is this moment gorgeous for your senses, but you can also experience moments of deeper relaxation, allowing for a greater connection to your entire energy systems where memory, information, and problem solving resides.

Ketheric Body Energy Field

Ancient philosophy teachings say there is a suspended energy surrounding all living objects on this earth. It acts as an 'energetic library' where all the information about your soul and previous lifetimes is held. This energy is known as 'The Akashic Records'. The Akashic Records are accessible through your 7th energy field, known as the Ketheric Body Energy Field, and your 7th chakra, The Crown Chakra, also known as the Brahmarandhra, at the very top of your head,

When the ketheric body energy field is blocked the information within the akashic records is typically out of reach. Absorbed healthy energy cannot freely flow through your body, there are delays of communication signals between your brain and body resulting in general poor well-being. Poor diet, lack of sleep, poor air quality, and of course stress blocks the ketheric body energy field.

A balanced ketheric body energy field is believed to open your sense of connection to other energies. Ancient Eastern philosophy regards an open, balanced ketheric body energy field as the reason for living life with a strong sense that everything is divinely orchestrated and designed to eventually work out for your highest good, where you receive information from your higher guidance. Some people regard this as karma, or the wheel of dharma. Others regard it as life lessons toward personal development.

Also known as the 'Protective Layer', this 7th aura regulates a constant flow of energy throughout your whole energetic and physical body. Both the crown chakra and the ketheric body energy field support the lower six energy fields by preventing energy leakage and unhealthy energy absorption.

Maintaining a balanced ketheric body energy field is necessary for achieving inner peace, connection to the higher self, and realising a clear sense of purpose. The way to bring awareness to your 7th aura is simple: create connections with like-minded individuals, where you can reflect on your beliefs, values, and purpose in life without judgement or criticism.

It is from this energy field that the entire matrix of energy systems are held together. It resembles the shape of an egg around the whole physical body, approximately 3 feet away from the skin. When the energy from the lower six energy fields are in optimum wellness, the internal body vibrations are said to 'burst' through the brahmarandhra, resonating golden threads of light.

To help your lower six energy fields and chakras balance in optimal wellness, and to assist your brahmarandhra in connecting to your akashic records, try these practices:

- **'Be open to new experiences'**: Expanding your horizons through new experiences can help clear your perspective and challenge how your habitual thoughts are inclined. Travel more, engage in new cultures, explore different studies, expose yourself to new ideas where you can step outside of your comfort just a little bit to feel the appreciation for something else.

- **Positive affirmations:** "I am consciously living my greater purpose from a place of love".

- **Read:** 30 minutes reading per day is thought have a massive positive impact on stress levels, improve sleep patterns, and give a gentle escape from the daily 'norm'.

Ultimately though, for the energy at the crown chakra and the ketheric body energy field to be balanced and harmonious, and therefore supportive to the nervous system and endocrine system, it is good practise to engage in energy cleansing movement that promotes circulation and makes you feel good – you know, the kind of exercise that makes you warm and mildly out of breath, that you could perhaps engage in with another like-minded person... I'll leave it to you to decide what exercise that could be (wink wink).

Life Energy

Good quality food, good quality air, and good quality people that you share values with are all incredibly powerful for the functioning of your energy systems and their associated emotions.

Ancient Eastern traditions followed a simple and logical philosophy to optimal health and well-being based on good digestion and the proper metabolism of food. These ancient Eastern lores are simple and easy to incorporate into daily eating habits:

When selecting & prepping your food:

- Choose high energy foods – organic and local when possible;
- Favour food that is properly cooked- ideally not raw and also not overly cooked in order to preserve the energetic life-force of the food;
- Favour high quality foods, fresh whenever possible and eat them before the use by date;
- Incorporate all five tastes in each meal: sweet, salty, sour, pungent, and bitter.

Food habits to favour... eat food:

- Fresh, ideally within 4 hours of preparation;
- In a settled, harmonious environment free of distractions;
- In a peaceful state of mind;
- In a sitting position;
- Only when you're hungry;
- At a moderate pace;
- At regular times;
- At an interval of 2-4 hours after a light meal or 4-6 hours after a full meal;

- Only till two-thirds capacity
- With gratitude for the food you receive and give praise for the cook

In addition:
- Allow 2-3 hours between eating and going to bed;
- Remain seated for a few minutes after completing your meal.

Types of foods to avoid (because they create sluggish digestion, tiredness, and overall imbalance and disease over time):

- Leftovers, especially ones over 24 hours;
- Frozen food;
- Improper combination of foods (listed below);
- Foods that are cooked in a negative environment;
- Deep- fried foods;
- Canned food;
- Microwaved foods;
- Foods with added preservatives.

Food combinations to avoid (because they change your body's PH acid alkaline balance):

- Milk or heavy cream with tomatoes, potatoes, aubergine, peppers, eggs, salt, fruit;
- Yoghurt with cheese or citrus fruits;
- Yoghurt with tomatoes, potatoes, aubergine, peppers, eggs, milk, or leafy greens;
- Cheese with fruit, tomatoes, potatoes, aubergine, peppers, meat, bread, crackers, macaroni, beans, or eggs;
- Meat and fish with eggs or dairy;
- Cucumber with lemon or lemon juice;
- Raw fruit with any other food;
- Oats with other foods.

Food habits to avoid or limit:

- Consuming foods under stress, while on the run or in a moving vehicle;
- Consuming foods when feeling very emotional as it will feed and grow that emotion;
- Drinking ice water because it decreases the digestive fire;
- Eating late at night;
- Falling asleep right after eating.

Universal Self Care

Your body is constantly communicating with the energies surrounding you. Every chakra preserves the pranic energy (universal energy) in your qi energy (life force energy) and jing energy (life essence energy) influencing your Shen energy (your shine).

Now that you understand the interconnectedness between your mind, body, and soul, it is essential to begin exploring the ways to balance and harmonise them – ways that work for you. By understanding and nurturing the energetic connections you can quickly and easily adopt daily practises that reduce stress, manage emotional and physical imbalances, and gain mental balance.

Remember to pay attention to hormonal health and the balance of your chakras as they work together to align the energy systems that make you. Here is a reminder of each chakra and what they do:

Root chakra is the foundation for life. As the first chakra it is located at the base of your tail bone. Connected to your Etheric Body Energy Field, both store emotional stress and feelings of being safe and rooted.
Shows as pelvis region discomfort = the deep lower back, top of thighs, and pelvic floor area.
The Stomach and Spleen energy channels control the secretion of adrenaline and cortisol hormones.

Virtue = faith and loyalty.
Vice = greed.
Basic need = survival (financial and material).

Sacral chakra seeks pleasure and enjoyment. As the second chakra it is located between your belly button and pubic bone. Connected to your Emotional Body Energy Field, they both store primitive feelings and emotional reaction patterns.
Shows as lumbar region discomfort = the lower back, hips, and belly area.
The Kidneys and Bladder energy channels control the secretion of Oestrogen, Progesterone and Testosterone hormones.

Virtue = charity.
Vice = lust.
Basic need = safety and security.

Solar Plexus is all about nourishment. As the third chakra it is located in the V of your ribcage. Connected to your Mental Body Energy Field, they both store want feelings and mental processes.
Shows as lower leg region discomfort = below the knee, calf, shin and ankle area.
The Heart and Small Intestine energy channels control the secretion of Insulin and Glucagon hormones.

Virtue = temperance / balance.
Vice = gluttony.
Basic need = belonging.

Heart chakra is the bridge between internal and external energies. As the fourth chakra it is located at your sternum. Connected to your Astral Body Energy Field, they both store patterns of how you adapt to change and your ability to give and receive unconditional love.
Shows as thoracic region discomfort = the chest and upper

back area.
The Lungs and Large Intestine energy channels control the secretion of Anti-Diuretic Hormones that control the amount of water and salt in your body.

Virtue = kindness.
Vice = jealousy.
Basic need = self-protection.

Throat chakra houses your ability to self-regulate and how you communicate with the world. As the fifth chakra it is located at your throat. Connected to your Etheric Template Energy Field, they both store need feelings and your ability to express yourself.
Shows as cervical region discomfort = the throat, neck, jaw, and ears.
The Liver and Galbladder energy channels control the secretion of Thyroxine and Triiodothyronine hormones that control your metabolism.

Virtue = courage.
Vice = fear or deep worry.
Basic need = self-actualisation.

Third Eye chakra is related to the awareness of more than yourself – the eye that sees and knows all. As the sixth chakra it is located in the centre of your two eyebrows. Connected to your Celestial Body Energy Field, they both filter external stresses and energetic chaos.
Shows as cervical region discomfort = the neck, face and skull areas.
The Tripple Burner and Pericardium energy channels control

the pituitary gland and the production of hormones including adrenaline, oestrogen, progesterone, testosterone, insulin and antidiuretic hormones.

Virtue = integrity.
Vice = laziness.
Basic need = self-reflection.

Crown chakra symbolisies trust and acceptance, and holds and harmonises all the other energy systems together. As the seventh chakra it is located at the very top centre of your head. Connected to your Ketheric Template Energy Field, they both store the blueprint of your soul's path and essentially guides you on your life's journey.

Virtue = humility.
Vice = pride.
Basic need = good quality people surrounding you.

The Link Between Your Inner World and Your Outer World

Once upon a time I sat with a yogic monk. A shift happened within me after meeting him. He hosted a group of talks where guidance was offered on how to get deep into the root of who we are, giving me an opportunity to really self-reflect. Below are the notes I wrote down from his teachings:

Wisdom of Eastern philosophy tells us the tensions in the body and the mind have a corresponding energetic tension, and vice versa. Eastern philosophy also tells us the purpose of the conscious mind is to influence, integrate, and harmonise all the levels of being. It is thought there are five levels of the conscious mind:

1. Ignorance of what is right and wrong
2. Attachment to knowledge, or a delusion of reality
3. Being distracted
4. Being focused
5. Pure consciousness

Ancient Eastern philosophy teachings say the most important part of life is to have a well-functioning body and a balanced mind. Purifying the body harmonises the hormone secretions which in turn balances the body, balances the mind, and balances the energies. But today's fast-paced standard of living creates an overflow of emotions due to an overflow of hormone secretions from the signals of the brain, and therefore an overwhelm of different frequency energies.

We can keep the mind, body, and soul balanced and functioning well by:

- Understanding the mind

- Understanding the energetic body: the roundabouts of energy [chakras], the roads of energy [energy channels], the vital energies [Prana, Qi, and Jing], the energies responsible for transformation, activation, and control [the endocrine glands and hormones], the energies responsible for the upright posture of the body and the ability to respond to the outside world [energy fields, also known as auras]; and
- Understanding that ordinary reality is not reality itself - remember we are never going to experience an event the same way as someone else.

Understanding the mind is about distinguishing between the conscious, subconscious, and unconscious mind. The conscious mind is the 'Crude Mind'. It works while we are awake. The subconscious mind is the 'Subtle Mind'. It is full of suppressed feelings, desires and emotions, which are expressed mostly during dream state. The unconscious mind is the 'Causal Mind'. It is not aware of this realm, but it awakens during deep sleep. This unconscious mind is the infinite self: the Soul.

If you go beyond the ego you will feel the flow of everlasting joy within the soul. This is done through what is said to be 'the revolution of consciousness', which is basically the expansion of the mind. Generally, in modern Western society, we are very much guided by narrowed sentiments where the mind is fickle and quick to change to suit certain feelings or situations. We have to control our ego to control our mind. Our mind is most of the time extroverted in thinking about what is going on externally. We have to change the flow of the mind from outward to inward. This is not easy... practise makes a person perfect.

We have to bring a revolution within ourselves and a revolution within society. What exactly is revolution? Revolution is a radical change: a complete change. We have to change our way of thinking... Then we can attain the real purpose of life, and begin to find a real answer for the big question: Who am I?

My answer: ...
"I AM A BUNDLE OF ENERGY."

I am a bundle of energy working with energy. I am life.

Who are you?

"Two roads diverged in a wood, and I took the one less travelled by. And that has made all the difference." – Robert Frost

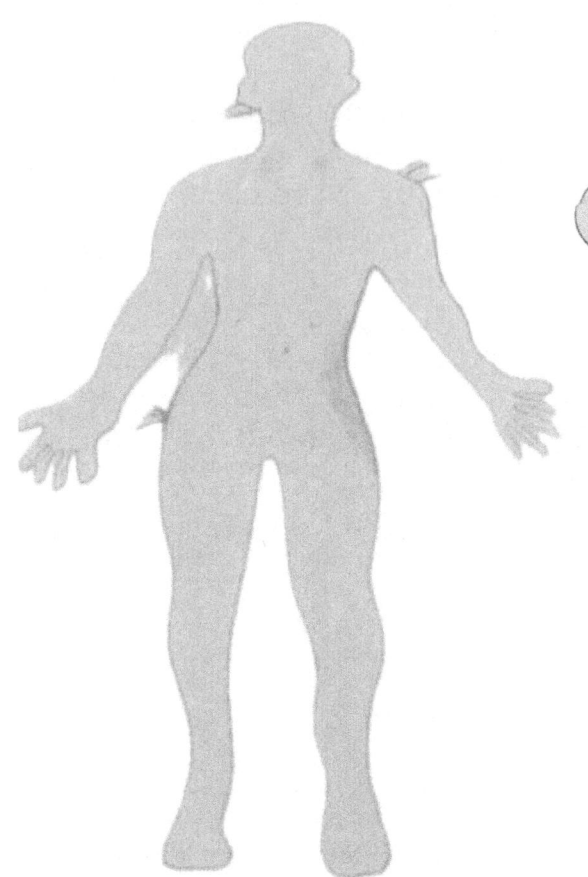

Make time in your day to do nothing – become aware of the sensations, feelings, and needs of your body in the present moment

Move your Body

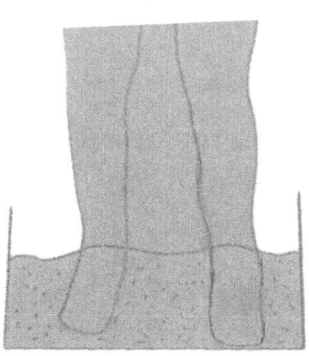

Give your feet a lovely soak in Magnesium Sulphate bath salts

Be with like-minded people

The Chakra of Enlightenment
<u>The Crown Chakra</u>
Your ability to understand how love, compassion, empathy, and forgiveness brings knowledge, wisdom, and bliss

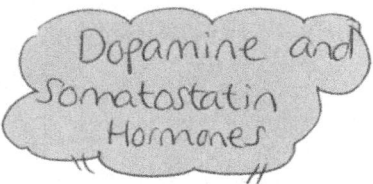

<u>*It Is About How You Foster Positive Social Interactions*</u>

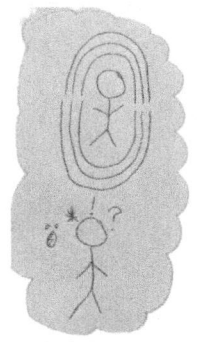

Everything will work out for the better?

OR

Everything is a problem and causes difficulties?

Feel Good

The Ketheric Body Energy Field can be seen as a constant flow of energy protecting energy leakage or unhealthy energy absorption

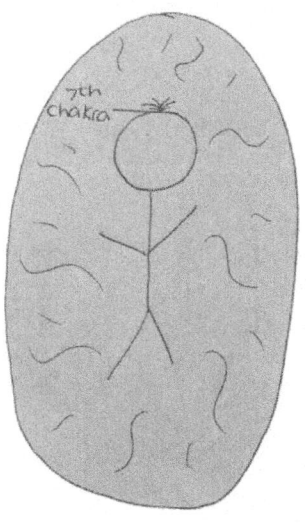

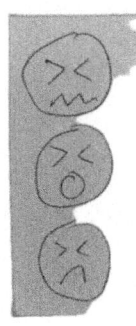

Your mind is full... you find settling the mind a challenge

Unsure of your purpose in life

Regularly experience random and short lived illnesses

Scents of patchouli and frankincense

Gold colours and good quality foods

Silence

"In tranquil moments, when the mind rests upon the shores of serenity, it unfurls its luminous wings. This inner radiance, unbounded and immeasurable, extends beyond the veil of our existence, casting its glow across the cosmic expanse."
- Unknown

Printed in Dunstable, United Kingdom